Innovation
And Thought Leadership In
Self-Driving Driverless Cars

Practical Advances in Artificial Intelligence (AI) and Machine Learning

Dr. Lance B. Eliot, MBA, PhD

DEDICATION

To my wonderful son, Michael, and my wonderful daughter, Lauren.

Forest fortuna adiuvat (from the Latin; good fortune favors the brave).

CONTENTS

Lance B. Eliot

ACKNOWLEDGMENTS

I have been the beneficiary of advice and counsel by many friends, colleagues, family, investors, and many others. I want to thank everyone that has aided me throughout my career. I write from the heart and the head, having experienced first-hand what it means to have others around you that support you during the good times and the tough times.

To Warren Bennis, one of my doctoral advisors and ultimately a colleague, I offer my deepest thanks and appreciation, especially for his calm and insightful wisdom and support.

To Mark Stevens and his generous efforts toward funding and supporting the USC Stevens Center for Innovation.

To Lloyd Greif and the USC Lloyd Greif Center for Entrepreneurial Studies for their ongoing encouragement of founders and entrepreneurs.

To Peter Drucker, William Wang, Aaron Levie, Peter Kim, Jon Kraft, Cindy Crawford, Jenny Ming, Steve Milligan, Chis Underwood, Frank Gehry, and Colonel Sanders, Buzz Aldrin, Steve Forbes, Bill Thompson, Dave Dillon, Alan Fuerstman, Larry Ellison, Jim Sinegal, John Sperling, Mark Stevenson, Anand Nallathambi, Thomas Barrack, Jr., and many other innovators and leaders that I have met and gained mightily from doing so.

Thanks to Ed Trainor, Kevin Anderson, James Hickey, Wendell Jones, Ken Harris, DuWayne Peterson, Mike Brown, Jim Thornton, Abhi Beniwal, Al Biland, John Nomura, Eliot Weinman, John Desmond, and many others for their unwavering support during my career.

And most of all thanks as always to Lauren and Michael, for their ongoing support and for having seen me writing and heard much of this material during the many months involved in writing it. To their patience and willingness to listen.

INTRODUCTION

This is a book that provides state-of-the-art innovations and the latest in "Thought Leadership" about the emerging nature of self-driving driverless cars. Via recent advances in Artificial Intelligence (AI) and Machine Learning (ML), we are nearing the day when vehicles can control themselves and will not require and nor rely upon human intervention to perform their driving tasks (or, that <u>allow</u> for human intervention, but only *require* human intervention in very limited ways).

Similar to my two other related books, which I describe in a moment and list the chapters in the Appendix A of this book, I am particularly focused on those advances that pertain to self-driving cars. The phrase "autonomous vehicles" is often used to refer to any kind of vehicle, whether it is ground-based or in the air or sea, and whether it is a cargo hauling trailer truck or a conventional passenger car. Though the aspects described in this book are certainly applicable to all kinds of autonomous vehicles, I am focused more so here on cars.

Indeed, I am especially known for my role in aiding the advancement of self-driving cars, serving currently as the Executive Director of the Cybernetic Self-Driving Cars Institute.. In addition to writing software, designing and developing systems and software for self-driving cars, I also speak and write quite a bit about the topic. This book is a collection of some of my more advanced essays. For those of you that might have seen my essays posted elsewhere, I have updated them and integrated them into this book as one handy cohesive package.

You might be interested in two companion books that I have written that cover additional key innovations and fundamentals about self-driving cars. One of those books is entitled "**Advances in AI and Autonomous Vehicles: Cybernetic Self-Driving Cars**," and the other is somewhat provocatively entitled **Self-Driving Cars: "The Mother of All AI Projects"** and which gained its title by the aspect that the CEO of Apple proclaimed that developing a self-driving car is "the mother of all AI projects," and is something I've been saying for many years. See Appendix A of this herein book to see a listing of the chapters covered in those two books.

For the introduction here to this book, I am going to borrow my introduction from those companion books, since it does a good job of laying out the landscape of self-driving cars and my overall viewpoints on the topic. The remainder of the book is all new material that does not appear in the companion books.

INTRODUCTION TO SELF-DRIVING CARS

This is a book about self-driving cars. Someday in the future, we'll all have self-driving cars and this book will perhaps seem antiquated, but right now, we are at the forefront of the self-driving car wave. Daily news bombards us with flashes of new announcements by one car maker or another and leaves the impression that within the next few weeks or maybe months that the self-driving car will be here. A casual non-technical reader would assume from these news flashes that in fact we must be on the cusp of a true self-driving car.

Here's a real news flash: We are still quite a distance from having a true self-driving car. It is years to go before we get there.

Why is that? Because a true self-driving car is akin to a moonshot. In the same manner that getting us to the moon was an incredible feat, likewise can it be said for achieving a true self-driving car. Anybody that suggests or even brashly states that the true self-driving car is nearly here should be viewed with great skepticism. Indeed, you'll see that I often tend to use the word "hogwash" or "crock" when I assess much of the decidedly *fake news* about self-driving cars. Those of us on the inside know that what is often reported to the outside is malarkey. Few of the insiders are willing to say so. I have no such hesitation.

Indeed, I've been writing a popular blog post about self-driving cars and hitting hard on those that try to wave their hands and pretend that we are on the imminent verge of true self-driving cars. For many years, I've been known as the AI Insider. Besides writing about AI, I also develop AI software. I do what I describe. It also gives me insights into what others that are doing AI are really doing versus what it is said they are doing.

Many faithful readers had asked me to pull together my insightful short essays and put them into another book, which you are now holding in your hands.

For those of you that have been reading my essays over the years, this collection not only puts them together into one handy package, I also updated the essays and added new material. For those of you that are new to the topic of self-driving cars and AI, I hope you find these essays approachable and informative. I also tend to have a writing style with a bit of a voice, and so you'll see that I am times have a wry sense of humor and also like to poke at conformity.

As a former professor and founder of an AI research lab, I for many years wrote in the formal language of academic writing. I published in referred journals and served as an editor for several AI journals. This writing here is not of the nature, and I have adopted a different and more informal style for these essays. That being said, I also do mention from time-to-time more rigorous material on AI and encourage you all to dig into those deeper and more formal materials if so interested.

I am also an AI practitioner. This means that I write AI software for a living. Currently, I head-up the Cybernetics Self-Driving Car Institute, where we are developing AI software for self-driving cars. I am excited to also report that my son, also a software engineer, heads-up our Cybernetics Self-Driving Car Lab. What I have helped to start, and for which he is an integral part, ultimately he will carry long into the future after I have retired. My daughter, a marketing whiz, also is integral to our efforts as head of our Marketing group. She too will carry forward the legacy now being formulated.

For those of you that are reading this book and have a penchant for writing code, you might consider taking a look at the open source code available for self-driving cars. This is a handy place to start learning how to develop AI for self-driving cars. There are also many new educational courses spring forth.

There is a growing body of those wanting to learn about and develop self-driving cars, and a growing body of colleges, labs, and other avenues by which you can learn about self-driving cars.

This book will provide a foundation of aspects that I think will get you ready for those kinds of more advanced training opportunities. If you've already taken those classes, you'll likely find these essays especially interesting as they offer a perspective that I am betting few other instructors or faculty offered to you. These are challenging essays that ask you to think beyond the conventional about self-driving cars.

THE MOTHER OF ALL AI PROJECTS

In June 2017, Apple CEO Tim Cook came out and finally admitted that Apple has been working on a self-driving car. As you'll see in my essays, Apple was enmeshed in secrecy about their self-driving car efforts. We have only been able to read the tea leaves and guess at what Apple has been up to. The notion of an iCar has been floating for quite a while, and self-driving engineers and researchers have been signing tight-lipped Non-Disclosure Agreements (NDA's) to work on projects at Apple that were as shrouded in mystery as any military invasion plans might be.

Tim Cook said something that many others in the Artificial Intelligence (AI) field have been saying, namely, the creation of a self-driving car has got to be the mother of all AI projects. In other words, it is in fact a tremendous moonshot for AI. If a self-driving car can be crafted and the AI works as we hope, it means that we have made incredible strides with AI and that therefore it opens many other worlds of potential breakthrough accomplishments that AI can solve.

Is this hyperbole? Am I just trying to make AI seem like a miracle worker and so provide self-aggrandizing statements for those of us writing the AI software for self-driving cars? No, it is not hyperbole. Developing a true self-driving car is really, really, really hard to do. Let me take a moment to explain why. As a side note, I realize that the Apple CEO is known for at times uttering hyperbole, and he had previously said for example that the year 2012 was "the mother of all years," and he had said that the release of iOS 10 was "the mother of all releases" – all of which does suggest he likes to use the handy "mother of" expression. But, I assure you, in terms of true self-driving cars, he has hit the nail on the head. For sure.

When you think about a moonshot and how we got to the moon, there are some identifiable characteristics and those same aspects can be applied to creating a true self-driving car. You'll notice that I keep putting the word "true" in front of the self-driving car expression. I do so because as per my essay about the various levels of self-driving cars (see Chapter 3), there are some self-driving cars that are only somewhat of a self-driving car. The somewhat versions are ones that require a human driver to be ready to intervene. In my view, that's not a true self-driving car. A true self-driving car is one that requires no human driver intervention at all. It is a car that can entirely undertake via automation the driving task without any human driver needed. This is the essence of what is known as a Level 5 self-driving car. We are currently at the Level 2 and Level 3 mark, and not yet at Level 5.

Getting to the moon involved aspects such as having big stretch goals, incremental progress, experimentation, innovation, and so on. Let's review how this applied to the moonshot of the bygone era, and how it applies to the self-driving car moonshot of today.

Big Stretch Goal

Trying to take a human and deliver the human to the moon, and bring them back, safely, was an extremely large stretch goal at the time. No one knew whether it could be done. The technology wasn't available yet. The cost was huge. The determination would need to be fierce. Etc. To reach a Level 5 self-driving car is going to be the same. It is a big stretch goal. We can readily get to the Level 3, and we are able to see the Level 4 just up ahead, but a Level 5 is still an unknown as to if it is doable. It should eventually be doable and in the same way that we thought we'd eventually get to the moon, but when it will occur is a different story.

Incremental Progress

Getting to the moon did not happen overnight in one fell swoop. It took years and years of incremental progress to get there. Likewise for self-driving cars. Google has famously been striving to get to the Level 5, and pretty much been willing to forgo dealing with the intervening levels, but most of the other self-driving car makers are doing the incremental route. Let's get a good Level 2 and a somewhat Level 3 going. Then, let's improve the Level 3 and get a somewhat Level 4 going. Then, let's improve the Level 4 and finally arrive at a Level 5. This seems to be the prevalent way that we are going to achieve the true self-driving car.

Experimentation

You likely know that there were various experiments involved in perfecting the approach and technology to get to the moon. As per making incremental progress, we first tried to see if we could get a rocket to go into space and safety return, then put a monkey in there, then with a human, then we went all the way to the moon but didn't land, and finally we arrived at the mission that actually landed on the moon. Self-driving cars are the same way. We are doing simulations of self-driving cars. We do testing of self-driving cars on private land under controlled situations. We do testing of self-driving cars on public roadways, often having to meet regulatory requirements including for example having an engineer or equivalent in the car to take over the controls if needed. And so on. Experiments big and small are needed to figure out what works and what doesn't.

Innovation

There are already some advances in AI that are allowing us to progress toward self-driving cars (see Chapter 1). We are going to need even more advances. Innovation in all aspects of technology are going to be required to achieve a true self-driving car. By no means do we already have everything in-hand that we need to get there. Expect new inventions and new approaches, new algorithms, etc.

Setbacks

Most of the pundits are avoiding talking about potential setbacks in the progress toward self-driving cars. Getting to the moon involved many setbacks, some of which you never have heard of and were buried at the time so as to not dampen enthusiasm and funding for getting to the moon. A recurring theme in many of my included essays is that there are going to be setbacks as we try to arrive at a true self-driving car. Take a deep breath and be ready. I just hope the setbacks don't completely stop progress. I am sure that it will cause progress to alter in a manner that we've not yet seen in the self-driving car field. I liken the self-driving car of today to the excitement everyone had for Uber when it first got going. Today, we have a different view of Uber and with each passing day there are more regulations to the ride sharing business and more concerns raised. The darling child only stays a darling until finally that child acts up. It will happen the same with self-driving cars.

SELF-DRIVING CARS CHALLENGES

But what exactly makes things so hard to have a true self-driving car, you might be asking. You have seen cruise control for years and years. You've lately seen cars that can do parallel parking. You've seen YouTube videos of Tesla drivers that put their hands out the window as their car zooms along the highway, and seen to therefore be in a self-driving car. Aren't we just needing to put a few more sensors onto a car and then we'll have in-hand a true self-driving car? Nope.

Consider for a moment the nature of the driving task. We don't just let anyone at any age drive a car. Worldwide, most countries won't license a driver until the age of 18, though many do allow a learner's permit at the age of 15 or 16. Some suggest that a younger age would be physically too small to reach the controls of the car. Though this might be the case, we could easily adjust the controls to allow for younger aged and thus smaller stature. It's not their physical size that matters. It's their cognitive development that matters.

To drive a car, you need to be able to reason about the car, what the car can and cannot do. You need to know how to operate the car. You need to know about how other cars on the road drive. You need to know what is allowed in driving such as speed limits and driving within marked lanes. You need to be able to react to situations and be able to avoid getting into accidents. You need to ascertain when to hit your brakes, when to steer clear of a pedestrian, and how to keep from ramming that motorcyclist that just cut you off.

Many of us had taken courses on driving. We studied about driving and took driver training. We had to take a test and pass it to be able to drive. The point being that though most adults take the driving task for granted, and we often "mindlessly" drive our cars, there is a significant amount of cognitive effort that goes into driving a car. After a while, it becomes second nature. You don't especially think about how you drive, you just do it. But, if you watch a novice driver, say a teenager learning to drive, you suddenly realize that there is a lot more complexity to it than we seem to realize.

Furthermore, driving is a very serious task. I recall when my daughter and son first learned to drive. They are both very conscientious people. They wanted to make sure that whatever they did, they did well, and that they did not harm anyone. Every day, when you get into a car, it is probably around 4,000 pounds of hefty metal and plastics (about two tons), and it is a lethal weapon. Think about it. You drive down the street in an object that weighs two tons and with the engine it can accelerate and ram into anything you want to hit. The damage a car can inflict is very scary. Both my children were surprised that they were being given the right to maneuver this monster of a beast that could cause tremendous harm entirely by merely letting go of the steering wheel for a moment or taking your eyes off the road.

In fact, in the United States alone there are about 30,000 deaths per year by auto accidents, which is around 100 per day. Given that there are about 263 million cars in the United States, I am actually more amazed that the number of fatalities is not a lot higher. During my morning commute, I look at all the thousands of cars on the freeway around me, and I think that if all of them decided to go zombie and drive in a crazy maniac way, there would be many people dead. Somehow, incredibly, each day, most people drive relatively safely. To me, that's a miracle right there. Getting millions and millions of people to be safe and sane when behind the wheel of a two ton mobile object, it's a feat that we as a society should admire with pride.

So, hopefully you are in agreement that the driving task requires a great deal of cognition. You don't' need to be especially smart to drive a car, and we've done quite a bit to make car driving viable for even the average dolt. There isn't an IQ test that you need to take to drive a car. If you can read and write, and pass a test, you pretty much can legally drive a car. There are of course some that drive a car and are not legally permitted to do so, plus there are private areas such as farms where drivers are young, but for public roadways in the United States, you can be generally of average intelligence (or less) and be able to legally drive.

This though makes it seem like the cognitive effort must not be much. If the cognitive effort was truly hard, wouldn't we only have Einstein's that could drive a car? We have made sure to keep the driving task as simple as we can, by making the controls easy and relatively standardized, and by having roads that are relatively standardized, and so on. It is as though Disneyland has put their Autopia into the real-world, by us all as a society agreeing that roads will be a certain way, and we'll all abide by the various rules of driving.

A modest cognitive task by a human is still something that stymies AI. You certainly know that AI has been able to beat chess players and be good at other kinds of games. This type of narrow cognition is not what car driving is about. Car driving is much wider. It requires knowledge about the world, which a chess playing AI system does not need to know. The cognitive aspects of driving are on the one hand seemingly simple, but at the same time require layer upon layer of knowledge about cars, people, roads, rules, and a myriad of other "common sense" aspects. We don't have any AI systems today that have that same kind of breadth and depth of awareness and knowledge.

As revealed in my essays, the self-driving car of today is using trickery to do particular tasks. It is all very narrow in operation. Plus, it currently assumes that a human driver is ready to intervene. It is like a child that we have taught to stack blocks, but we are needed to be right there in case the child stacks them too high and they begin to fall over. AI of today is brittle, it is narrow, and it does not approach the cognitive abilities of humans. This is why the true self-driving car is somewhere out in the future.

Another aspect to the driving task is that it is not solely a mind exercise. You do need to use your senses to drive. You use your eyes a vision sensors to see the road ahead. You vision capability is like a streaming video, which your brain needs to continually analyze as you drive. Where is the road? Is there a pedestrian in the way? Is there another car ahead of you? Your senses are relying a flood of info to your brain. Self-driving cars are trying to do the same, by using cameras, radar, ultrasound, and lasers. This is an attempt at mimicking how humans have senses and sensory apparatus.

Thus, the driving task is mental and physical. You use your senses, you use your arms and legs to manipulate the controls of the car, and you use your brain to assess the sensory info and direct your limbs to act upon the controls of the car. This all happens instantly. If you've ever perhaps gotten something in your eye and only had one eye available to drive with, you suddenly realize how dependent upon vision you are. If you have a broken foot with a cast, you suddenly realize how hard it is to control the brake pedal and the accelerator. If you've taken medication and your brain is maybe sluggish, you suddenly realize how much mental strain is required to drive a car.

An AI system that plays chess only needs to be focused on playing chess. The physical aspects aren't important because usually a human moves the chess pieces or the chessboard is shown on an electronic display. Using AI for a more life-and-death task such as analyzing MRI images of patients, this again does not require physical capabilities and instead is done by examining images of bits.

Driving a car is a true life-and-death task. It is a use of AI that can easily and at any moment produce death. For those colleagues of mine that are developing this AI, as am I, we need to keep in mind the somber aspects of this. We are producing software that will have in its virtual hands the lives of the occupants of the car, and the lives of those in other nearby cars, and the lives of nearby pedestrians, etc. Chess is not usually a life-or-death matter.

Driving is all around us. Cars are everywhere. Most of today's AI applications involve only a small number of people. Or, they are behind the scenes and we as humans have other recourse if the AI messes up. AI that is driving a car at 80 miles per hour on a highway had better not mess up. The consequences are grave. Multiply this by the number of cars, if we could put magically self-driving into every car in the USA, we'd have AI running in the 263 million cars. That's a lot of AI spread around. This is AI on a massive scale that we are not doing today and that offers both promise and potential peril.

There are some that want AI for self-driving cars because they envision a world without any car accidents. They envision a world in which there is no car congestion and all cars cooperate with each other. These are wonderful utopian visions.

They are also very misleading. The adoption of self-driving cars is going to be incremental and not overnight. We cannot economically just junk all existing cars. Nor are we going to be able to affordably retrofit existing cars. It is more likely that self-driving cars will be built into new cars and that over many years of gradual replacement of existing cars that we'll see the mix of self-driving cars become substantial in the real-world.

In these essays, I have tried to offer technological insights without being overly technical in my description, and also blended the business, societal, and economic aspects too. Technologists need to consider the non-technological impacts of what they do. Non-technologists should be aware of what is being developed.

We all need to work together to collectively be prepared for the enormous disruption and transformative aspects of true self-driving cars. We all need to be involved in this mother of all AI projects.

WHAT THIS BOOK PROVIDES

What does this book provide to you? It introduces many of the key elements about self-driving cars and does so with an AI based perspective. I weave together technical and non-technical aspects, readily going from being concerned about the cognitive capabilities of the driving task and how the technology is embodying this into self-driving cars, and in the next breath I discuss the societal and economic aspects.

They are all intertwined because that's the way reality is. You cannot separate out the technology per se, and instead must consider it within the milieu of what is being invented and innovated, and do so with a mindset towards the contemporary mores and culture that shape what we are doing and what we hope to do.

TOUR OF THIS BOOK

Let's do a quick tour of this book.

In Chapter 1, I take a look at sensor fusion for self-driving cars. A self-driving car has numerous sensory devices, such as radar, cameras, and the like, and the data that is streaming real-time from those devices needs to be quickly examined and transformed into something that the AI system can make use of. This processing of sensory data is known as sensor fusion. If sensor fusion is done well, it helps to assure that the AI is getting the right info that it needs to render sound decisions. If the sensor fusion is poorly done, it can lead to misleading indications to the AI that will then cause the AI to make unsound decisions.

In Chapter 2, street scene free space detection is discussed. This involves the analysis of sensory data to try and determine where there is available "free space," which means space that the self-driving car can potentially drive into. As you drive your own car, you are continually looking for free space, such as trying to find a spot ahead of you to change lanes, and so this is a fundamental aspect of the driving task.

In Chapter 3, I cover a topic that few others are discussing, namely the importance of self-awareness for self-driving cars. A self-driving car needs to be continually considering its own status. Is it driving the car well? Are the sensors working properly? Just as a human has self-awareness, we need the AI of a self-driving car to act likewise.

In Chapter 4, there is a discussion about cartographic trade-offs of self-driving cars. This has to do with maps. How much does a self-driving car depend upon having a map? Some say that a self-driving car cannot proceed to drive without a map. I explore these aspects and explain the role that maps do have and how they do not necessarily impede a self-driving car per se.

In Chapter 5, I discuss toll road traversal for self-driving cars. When a self-driving car comes up to a toll road, there are aspects to the driving task that are unusual in comparison to the normal straight ahead driving tasks. I explain how this kind of "edge" problem of self-driving cars is being solved.

In Chapter 6, there is a discussion about predictive scenario modeling for self-driving cars. A self-driving car must be anticipating what will happen in the future. Is the road ahead usable, and if not, what should the self-driving car be prepared to do.

In Chapter 7, this is one of my favorite topics and one that no one else seems to be covering, namely, the role of selfishness in self-driving cars. I contend that any good self-driving car will ultimately need to have selfishness. Read this chapter and decide whether you agree or disagree with my arguments about that aspect.

In Chapter 8, there is an indication of what I call leap frog driving aspects for self-driving cars. You likely have done leap frog driving, and just didn't realize it was a thing. It involves switching lanes to get around another vehicle and then popping back into your lane. A common driving tactic. Some say that self-driving cars should not copy this approach, and that it is a bad habit of lousy drivers. I contend it is a fundamental aspect of driving and should not be ignored or set aside.

In Chapter 9, I discuss the proprioceptive Inertial Measurement Units (IMU's) that need to be inside a self-driving car. It is the internal compass, so to speak, and works hand-in-hand with the GPS.

In Chapter 10, when a person is hijacked via their car, it is commonly referred to as a carjacking. With the advent of self-driving cars, a new term has emerged, namely, it is now called robojacking. Learn about how this new form of crime will haunt us as we emerge into the era of self-driving cars.

In Chapter 11, I explain more of my thinking about why the development of a self-driving car is like a moonshot. I trace the aspects of what got us to the moon, and try to draw parallels to how we are now proceeding toward a self-driving car. You'll see that there are aspects in common, and other aspects that differ.

In Chapter 12, there is an innovative look at how marketing of cars will change because of self-driving cars. The ways in which cars are marketed today will need to change to accommodate no longer having human drivers as the focus for car advertising.

In Chapter 13, I compare the nature of airplane autopilot systems to the nature of self-driving cars. Many people ask me over and over whether or not these are really the same technologies. I explain why they differ and how they can each enrich the other.

In Chapter 14, it is vitally important that we all become much more aware of the importance of regulators and regulations that will impact the emergence of self-driving cars. There are some that say there should be almost no regulations, while others clamor for heavy regulations. I discuss the trade-offs of regulatory aspects. And, I also describe the tremendous work being done by Assemblyman Marc Berman, a regulator in the Silicon Valley area of California that has his finger on the pulse of self-driving cars.

In Chapter 15, I discuss a very serious topic, the role of Event Data Recorders (EDR's) for self-driving cars. These are the famous black boxes that you know about for airplanes. Right now, there is no regulation that requires that these EDR's be included in all self-driving cars. Plus, it is important that if an EDR is included that it be recording the kind of data that will be helpful when needed to understand what transpired prior to and during an accident involving a self-driving car.

In Chapter 16, the topic of looking behind a self-driving car is discussed. Some self-driving cars do not have sensors that look to determine what is behind the self-driving car, or have sensors that are no more than simple back-up cam like devices. I contend that a true self-driving car must take as seriously what is behind it as what is in front of it.

In Chapter 17, there is a discussion about in-car voice commands and the use of Natural Language Processing (NLP) for self-driving cars. This covers the aspects of how we as human occupants will interact with a self-driving car.

In Chapter 18, the topic of what needs to happen when a cop pulls over a self-driving car is discussed. Some are surprised to think that a cop would pull over a self-driving car. Shouldn't a self-driving car always be driving legally and so therefore never a need for a cop to pull it over? Wrong. There are lots of reasons that a cop might need to pull over a self-driving car. Plus, the self-driving car needs to legally abide by an officer of the law when it is asked to pull over.

In Chapter 19, I bring up a somewhat wild idea that you might think crazy. In a science fiction way, we are gradually getting better at connecting into the human brain to allow for a Brain Machine Interface (BMI) and commands from the brain to other worldly devices. This could well apply to self-driving cars.

WHY THIS BOOK

I wrote this book to try and bring to the public view many aspects about self-driving cars that nobody seems to be discussing.

For business leaders that are either involved in making self-driving cars or that are going to leverage self-driving cars, I hope that this book will enlighten you as to the risks involved and ways in which you should be strategizing about how to deal with those risks.

For entrepreneurs, startups and other businesses that want to enter into the self-driving car market that is emerging, I hope this book sparks your interest in doing so, and provides some sense of what might be prudent to pursue.

For researchers that study self-driving cars, I hope this book spurs your interest in the risks and safety issues of self-driving cars, and also nudges you toward conducting research on those aspects.

For students in computer science or related disciplines, I hope this book will provide you with interesting and new ideas and material, for which you might conduct research or provide some career direction insights for you.

For AI companies and high-tech companies pursuing self-driving cars, this book will hopefully broaden your view beyond just the mere coding and development needed to make self-driving cars.

For all readers, I hope that you will find the material in this book to be stimulating. Some of it will be repetitive of things you already know. But I am pretty sure that you'll also find various eureka moments whereby you'll discover a new technique or approach that you had not earlier thought of. I am also betting that there will be material that forces you to rethink some of your current practices.

I am not saying you will suddenly have an epiphany and change what you are doing. I do think though that you will reconsider or perhaps revisit what you are doing.

For anyone choosing to use this book for teaching purposes, please take a look at my suggestions for doing so, as described in the Appendix. I have found the material handy in courses that I have taught, and likewise other faculty have told me that they have found the material handy, in some cases as extended readings and in other instances as a core part of their course (depending on the nature of the class).

In my writing for this book, I have tried carefully to blend both the practitioner and the academic styles of writing. It is not as dense as is typical academic journal writing, but at the same time offers depth by going into the nuances and trade-offs of various practices.

The word "deep" is in vogue today, meaning getting deeply into a subject or topic, and so is the word "unpack" which means to tease out the underlying aspects of a subject or topic. I have sought to offer material that addresses an issue or topic by going relatively deeply into it and make sure that it is well unpacked.

Finally, in any book about AI, it is difficult to use our everyday words without having some of them be misinterpreted. Specifically, it is easy to anthropomorphize AI. When I say that an AI system "knows" something, I do not want you to construe that the AI system has sentience and "knows" in the same way that humans do. They aren't that way, as yet. I have tried to use quotes around such words from time-to-time to emphasize that the words I am using should not be misinterpreted to ascribe true human intelligence to the AI systems that we know of today. If I used quotes around all such words, the book would be very difficult to read, and so I am doing so judiciously. Please keep that in mind as you read the material, thanks.

COMPANION BOOKS

If you find this material of interest, you might want to also see my other two books on self-driving cars, one entitled *Self-Driving Cars: "The Mother of ALL AI Projects"* and the other entitled "**Advances in AI and Autonomous Vehicles: Cybernetic Self-Driving Cars**" both of which contain more of my at-times controversial and under-the-hood explorations about the nature of self-driving cars.

CHAPTER 1

SENSOR FUSION FOR SELF-DRIVING CARS

CHAPTER 1

SENSOR FUSION FOR SELF-DRIVING CARS

There are essentially three main system functions of self-driving cars: (1) car sensor-related system functions, (2) car processing related functions that we tend to consider the AI of the self-driving car, and (3) car control related functions that operate the accelerator, the brakes, the steering wheel, etc.

I am going to discuss today mainly the sensors and an important aspect of sensory data usage that is called sensor fusion. That being said, it is crucial to realize that all three of these main systems must work in coordination with each other. If you have the best sensors, but the AI and the control systems are wimpy then you won't have a good self-driving car. If you have lousy sensors and yet have strong AI and controls capabilities, you will once again have likely problems because without good sensors the car won't know what exists in the outside world as it drives and could ram into things.

As the Executive Director of the Cybernetic Self-Driving Car Institute, I am particularly interested in sensor fusion, and so I thought it might be handy to offer some insights on that particular topic. But, as noted above, keep in mind that the other systems and their functions are equally important to having a viable self-driving car.

A self-driving car needs to have sensors that detect the world, and there needs to be subsystems focused on dealing with the sensors and sensory data being collected. These can be sensors such as cameras that collect visual images, radar that makes use of radio waves to detect objects, LIDAR, that makes use of laser light waves, ultrasonic sensors

17

that use sound waves, and so on. There are passive sensors, such as the camera that merely accepts light into it and therefore receives images, and there are active sensors such as radar that sends out an electromagnetic radio wave and then receives back the bounce to then figure out whether an object was detected.

The sensory data needs to be put together in some fashion, referred to as sensor fusion, in order to make sense of the sensory data. Usually, the overarching AI processing system is maintaining a virtual model of the world within which the car is driving, and the model is updated by new data arriving from the sensors. As a result of the sensor fusion, the AI then needs to decide what actions should be undertaken, and then emits appropriate commands to the controls of the car to carry out those actions.

An apt analogy would be to the way that the human body works. Your eyes are receiving visual images. Those images are conveyed to your brain. Your brain has a mental model of the world around you. Based on the images, the brain updates the model. Using the model, the brain ascertains what your body should do next. Let's suppose you are in Barcelona and at the running of the bulls. You are standing on a street corner waiting for the madcap bulls to arrive. Your brain has a mental model of the streets and the people around you. Your eyes suddenly see the bulls charging toward you. The images of the charging bulls stream into your brain. Your brain updates the mental model of the situation, and determines that you ought to start running like mad. The brain then commands your legs to engage and start running. It directs them to run away from the bulls and down the street to try and escape them.

In this analogy, we had a sensor, your eyes. It was collecting visual images. The eyes themselves don't do much with the images per se. They are predominantly dealing with getting the images. There is some fault tolerance capabilities of your eyeballs, in that even if your eye is partially covered up you can still use it to capture images. Furthermore, if you eye gets occluded, let's say that you get something in your eye like a piece of lint, the eye is able to continue functioning but also realizes that something is amiss. This is transmitted to the brain. There isn't much image processing per se in the eyeball itself in terms of making sense of the image. The eyeball is not (at least as we know) figuring out that the creature running toward you is a bull. It is up the brain to take the raw images fed by the eyeballs

18

and try to figure out what the image consists of and its significance.

Your brain keeps a context of the existing situation around you. Standing there in Barcelona, your brain knows that your body is at the running of the bulls. It has a mental model that then can make good sense of the image of the charging bull, because your brain realizes that a charging bull is a likely scenario in this present world situation you find yourself in. Suppose that instead you were standing in New York Times Square. Your mental model would not likely include the chances of a charging bull coming at you. Your brain could still nonetheless process the aspect that a charging bull was coming at you, but it would not tend to fit into the mental model of the moment. You might be expecting a taxi to run at you, or maybe a nut wearing a spider-man outfit, but not probably a wild charging bull.

Humans have multiple senses. You take the sense of sight and your brain uses it to inform the mental model and make decisions. You also have the sense of touch, and ability to detect odors, the sense of taste, and the sense of hearing. There are various sensory devices on your body that pertain to these aspects. Your ears are your sensory devices for hearing of sounds. Those sounds are fed into the brain. The brain tries to figure out what those sounds mean. In the case of being in Barcelona, you might have heard the pounding hoofs of the bulls, prior to actually seeing the bulls coming around the corner. Your brain would have updated the mental model that the bulls are nearby. It might have then commanded your legs to start running. Or, it might opt to wait and determine whether your eyes can confirm that the bulls are charging at you. It might want to have a secondary set of sensory devices to reaffirm what the other sensory device reported.

On self-driving cars, there can be just one type of sensory device, let's say radar. This though would mean that the self-driving car has only one type of way of sensing the world. It would be akin to your having only your eyes and not having other senses like your ears. Thus, there can be multiple types of sensory devices on a self-driving cars, such as radar, LIDAR, and ultrasonic.

There are individual sensors and potentially multiples of those by type. For example, a Tesla might come equipped with one radar unit, hidden under the front grill, and then six ultrasonic units, dispersed around the car and mounted either on the outside of the skin of the car or just inside of it. Each of these types of sensors has a somewhat different purpose. Just as your eyes differ from your ears, so do these sensor types.

Radar for example is used for distance detection and speed of objects, typically at a range of around 500 feet or so. Ultrasonic sensors are usually used for very near distance detection, often within about 3 to 6 feet of the car. The radar would tend to be used for normal driving functions and trying to detect if there is a car ahead of the self-driving car. The ultrasonic sensors tend to be used when the self-driving car is parking, since it needs to know what is very nearby to the car, or can also be used when changing lanes while driving since it can try to detect other cars in your blind spot.

Recall that I mentioned that your eyes can do some amount of fault detection and have a range of fault tolerance. Likewise with the sensors on the self-driving car. A radar unit might realize that its electromagnetic waves are not being sent out and returned in a reliable manner. This could mean that the radar itself has a problem. Or, it could be that it is trying to detect an object beyond its normal functional range, let's say the stated range is 500 feet and there is an object at 600 feet. The radar wave returns from the object might be very weak. As such, the radar is not sure whether the object is really there or not. There can also be ghosting which involves situations whereby a sensor believes something is there when it is not. Think about how you sometimes are in a very dark room and believe that maybe you see an image floating in the air. Is it there or does your eyeball just get somewhat confused and falsely believe an image is there? The eyeball can play tricks on us and offer stimulation to the brain that is based on spurious aspects.

For self-driving cars, there have been some researchers who have purposely shown that it is possible to spoof the sensors on the self-driving car. They created images to trick the self-driving car camera into believing that the self-driving car was in a context that it was not (imagine if you were standing in Barcelona but I held up a picture of New York Times Square, your eyeballs would convey the image of New York Times Square and your brain needs to figure out what is going on, is it a picture or have you been transported Star Trek style into New York). Researchers have spoofed the radar. You might already know that for years there have been outlawed devices that some had in their cars to fool the radar guns used by police. The device would trick the radar gun into showing a speed that was much less than the speed of the actual driving car. Sorry, those were outlawed.

A sensor can produce what is considered a false positive. This is a circumstance involving a sensor that says something is present, but it is not. Suppose the radar reports that there is a car directly ahead of you and it is stopped in the road. The AI of the self-driving car might suddenly jam on the brakes. If the camera of the self-driving car is not showing an image of a car ahead of you, this conflicts with what the radar has said. The AI needs to ascertain which is correct, the radar reporting the object, or the images that don't show the object. Maybe the object is invisible to the camera, but visible to the radar. Or, maybe the radar is reporting a ghost and the radar should be ignored because the camera shows there is no object there. If the radar is correct and the object is there, but the camera doesn't show it to be there, the camera would be said to be reporting a false negative. A false negative consists of a sensor saying that something is not present when it actually is there.

Any of the sensors can at any time be reporting a false positive or a false negative. It is up to the AI of the self-driving car to try and figure out which is which. This can be hard to do. The AI will typically canvas all its sensors to try and determine whether any one sense is doing false reporting. Some AI systems will judge which sensor is right by pre-determining that some of the sensors are better than the others, or it might do a voting protocol wherein if X sensors vote that something is there and Y do not then if $X > Y$ by some majority that it will decide it is there. Another popular method is known as the Random Sample Consensus (RANSAC) approach. Risk is also used as a factor in that it might be safer to falsely come to a halt than it would be to risk ramming into an object that you weren't sure was there but it turns out is there.

This is where sensor fusion comes to play. Sensor fusion consists of collecting together sensory data and trying to make sense of it. In some cars, like certain models of the Tesla, there is a sensor fusion between the camera and the radar, and then this is fed into the AI of the car. The AI of the car then receives a combined sensor fusion from those two units, and must combine it with other sensory data such as the ultrasonic sensors. I mention this because there is not necessarily one central place of sensor fusion in a self-driving car. There can be multiple places of sensor fusion. This can be important to note. Imagine if your brain was receiving not the raw images of the eyes and the ears, but instead some pre-processed version of what your eyes and ears had detected. The sensor fusion in-the-middle is going to be making assumptions and transformations that then the brain becomes reliant upon.

Within the self-driving car, there is a network that allows for communication among the devices in the self-driving car. The Society for Automotive Engineers (SAE) has defined a handy standard known as C.A.N. (Controller Area Network). It is a network that does not need a host computer, and instead the devices on the network can freely send messages across the network. Devices on the network are supposed to be listening for messages, meaning they are watching to see if a message has come along intended for that device. The devices are usually called Electronic Control Units (ECU) and are considered nodes in this network. This CAN is similar to the TCP-IP protocol and allows for asynchronous communications among the devices, and each message is encompassed in an envelope that indicates an ID for the message along with error correcting codes and the message itself.

The sensor fusion is often referred to as Multi-Sensor Data Fusion (MSDF). By taking the data from multiple sensors, there is a low-level analysis done to ascertain which sensors are Ok and which might be having problems. The MSDF will have a paradigm or methodology that it is using to decide which sensors are perhaps faulty and which are not. It will ultimately then send along a transformed indication of the raw sensor data and also then some kind of conclusions about the sensory data, and push that along to the brains of the self-driving car, the AI. The AI system or processing system then updates the model of the environment and must decide what to do about it at a higher-level of abstraction. The outcome is typically a command to the controls of the car, such as to speed-up, slow down, turn left, turn right, etc.

The Field-of-View (FOV) of the self-driving car is vital to what it knows about the outside world. For example, a radar unit at the front grille of the car is typically going to have a fan-like wave of radar detection, but it is only with respect to what is directly in front of the car. Objects that are at off-angles of the car might not be detected by the radar. The radar is for sure not detecting what is behind the car and nor to the side of the car in this instance. The AI system needs to realize that the info coming from the radar is only providing a FOV directly ahead of the car. It is otherwise blind to what is behind the car and to the sides of the car.

LIDAR is often used in today's self-driving cars to create a 360-degree model of the surrounding environment. The LIDAR uses laser light pulses and often is made to rotate continuously in a 360-degree circle. By doing so, the LIDAR can provide object detection of objects completely around the car. When combined with the front-facing radar, and a front-facing camera, and ultrasonic sensors on the sides of the car, a more full-bodied world model can be constructed and maintained. You might wonder why not have a zillion such sensors on the self-driving car, which would presumably allow for an even more robust indication of the outside world. You could certainly do so, though it causes the cost of the car to rise, and the weight and size of the car to rise.

Self-driving car makers are all jockeying to figure out how many sensors, which sensors, and which combination of sensors makes sense for a self-driving car. More sensors, more data, more to process, more cost of hardware. Less sensors, less data, less to process, lower cost of hardware. As I have previously mentioned, Elon Musk of Tesla says he does not believe LIDAR is needed for self-driving cars, and so there is not LIDAR being used on Tesla's. Is he right or is he wrong? We don't yet know. Time will tell.

There is some point at which a self-driving car is safe or not safe, or safer versus not safer than another one. This is why I have been predicting that we are going to see a shake-up eventually in self-driving cars. Those that had chosen some combination of sensors that turns out to not be as safe are going to lose out. We don't know what the right equation is as yet. In theory, the testing of self-driving cars on public roadways is going to reveal this, though hopefully not at the cost of the loss of human lives.

Based on the sensor data, there is usually Multi-Target Tracking (MTT) that needs to be undertaken. The raw data needs to be examined to identify features and do what is known as feature extraction. From a camera image, the sensor fusion might determine that a pedestrian is standing a few feet away from the car. If there is concern that the pedestrian might walk into the path of the car, the AI might decide to track that pedestrian. Thus, as subsequent images are captured from the camera, the pedestrian becomes a "target" object that has been deemed to be worthy of tracking. If the pedestrian seems to be about to get run over, the AI might then task the brakes to do a hard-braking action.

There is a need for the AI system to consider the sensory data in both a spatial manner and a temporal manner. Spatially, the sensor data is indicating what is presumably physically around the car. There is a car ahead, a pedestrian to the right, and a wall to the left of the car. For temporal purposes, the AI needs to realize that things are changing over time. The pedestrian has now moved from the right of the car to the left of the car. The car ahead is no longer ahead since it has pulled to the side of the road and stopped. The AI is reviewing the sensory data in real-time, as it streams into the AI system, and besides having a spatial model of the objects it must also have a temporal model. Object in position A is moving toward position B, and if so, what should the self-driving car do once the object gets to position B.

Notice that the AI therefore needs to be aware of the present situation and also predicting the future. We do this as human drivers. I see a pedestrian, let's say a teenager on his skateboard. He's on the sidewalk and moving fast. I anticipate that he is going to jump off the curb and possibly intersect with the path of my car. I therefore decide to swerve in-advance to my left and avoid hitting him once he makes the jump. The AI of the self-driving car would have been receiving sensor data about the teenager and would have had to make the same kinds of predictions in the model of the world that it has.

For those of you that are aware of the speed of microprocessors, you might be right now wondering how can all of this massive amount of sensory data that is pouring in each split second be getting processed in real-time and quickly enough for the self-driving car to make the timely decisions that are needed.

You are absolutely right that this needs tremendously fast processors and a lot of them too, working in parallel. Let's trace things. There is a radar image captured, and the ECU for the radar unit does some pre-processing, which takes a split-second to do. It then sends that along the CAN to the sensor fusion. This takes time to travel on the network and be received. The sensor fusion is getting likewise data from the camera, from the ultrasonic, from the LIDAR. The sensor fusion processes all of this, which takes another split-second. The result is sent along to the AI. The AI needs to process it and update the world model. This takes time. The AI then sends a command to the controls of the car, which goes across the CAN network and takes time to happen. The controls then receive the command, determine what it says to do, and physically take action. This all takes time too.

If the processors are not fast enough, and if the lag time between the sensor data collection and the final act of telling the controls to engage is overly long, you could have a self-driving car that gets into an accident, killing someone.

Not only is it about the raw speed of the processors, but it is also what the processing itself is doing. If the AI, for example, deliberates overly long, it might have reached a correct decision but no longer have time to implement it. You've probably been in a car with a human driver that hesitated to try and make the change of light at an intersection. Their hesitation put them into a bind wherein they either try to rocket through the now red light or come to a screeching halt at the edge of the intersection. Either way, they have increased the risk to themselves and those around them, due to the hesitation. Self-driving cars can get themselves into exactly the same predicament.

Here's then some of the factors about sensors and sensor fusion that need to be considered:

- Cost
- Size
- Weight
- Scalability
- Reliability
- Cooling
- Mounting Space
- Self-Diagnosis
- Error Reporting
- Fault Tolerance
- Flexibility
- Redundancy
- Spoofness
- Etc.

Sensor fusion is a vital aspect of self-driving cars. For those of you who are software engineers or computer scientists, there are ample opportunities to provide new approaches and innovative methods to improving sensor fusion. Self-driving car makers know that good sensor fusion is essential to a well operating self-driving car. Most consumers have no clue that sensor fusion is taking place and nor how it is occurring. All they want to know is that the self-driving car is magical and able to safely take them from point Y to point Z. The better sensor fusion gets, the less obvious it will be, and yet the safer our self-driving cars will be.

CHAPTER 2

STREET SCENE FREE SPACE DETECTION FOR SELF-DRIVING CARS

CHAPTER 2

STREET SCENE FREE SPACE DETECTION FOR SELF-DRIVING CARS

Where is the road?

I was driving up in the mountains and gradually making my way to a hidden valley that I was told would be a remarkable sight to see. The mountains had the usual curving roads, going back and forth in a see-saw way. I was aware that some locals liked to really gun their engines on these mountainous roads, since they traveled them all the time and had become accustomed to knowing when the curve would switch one way or another. It was hard for me to tell that once I came out of a sharp left curve that I might suddenly need to enter into a sharp right curve. Coming around each of the tight bends, you couldn't see anything until you actually made the bend itself.

Admittedly, I was driving pretty slowly and carefully. I did not want to lose my life on some mountainous road. Even in spite of the fact that the road was leading me to a wondrous hidden valley. It was actually a Boy Scout campsite that few knew about other than the Boy Scout troops in the area. The location was ideal for scouting purposes. We could have the Boy Scouts seemingly be in the middle of nowhere and use their wilderness survival skills, and yet the camp was only about an hour outside of the highly populated city environment of Los Angeles.

For a moment, go ahead and close your eyes and imagine driving on a road that you could not see more than say 50 feet up ahead. You are approaching a tight curve. You can only see the road that is directly ahead of you. After it curves around the bend, you cannot see at all what happens to the road, not at least until you are fully committed into the bend and already have made most of the curve.

You are going to likely assume that the roadway past where you can see is just fine. In other words, you have to make the assumption that the road continues naturally after the bend. It is surface that is drivable. It is an intact road. The road is marked and properly maintained. Your car will be able to flow right onto that road portion. These are the aspects that you take for granted.

Suppose though that as you make the bend, you suddenly encounter a huge boulder which has fallen onto the roadway. It fell right into the worst possible location. It is sitting just after the bend. As you are making the curve before where the curve bends, you cannot see that a boulder is there. You will only see the boulder in the moments just as you make the bend. At that point, depending upon your speed, you might have maybe a split second to make a decision as to what to do. If the boulder occupies only your lane, maybe you can swing wide to avoid it. But, if you swing wide, maybe a car coming in the opposite direction will be in that lane and the two of you will collide head-on.

Suppose you anticipate that you would simply hit your brakes and stop before striking the boulder. That's handy, but let's walk through what needs to happen and the time it takes. Think about the amount of time needed to see the boulder, recognize it as a boulder, mentally calculate that it is obstructing your path, mentally calculate that there is no other recourse other than to hit the brakes, mentally command your foot to come off the accelerator pedal so you can switch it to the brakes, do so and have your foot them slam down on the brakes. How long does that take to do? If it takes more than a split second, which it most likely does, you will have already rammed into the boulder at full speed since the amount of time you had to do all that was only a split second.

You can likely understand why I was driving slowly and carefully. I was trying to avoid a situation whereby I encountered a problem up ahead of me that I could not foresee, and for which the faster I was going would reduce inch by inch and second by second my options for taking any needed evasive action. Of course, it could be something other than a large boulder. A large boulder is probably nifty as something that is awry simply because it would be easily identified and instantly recognizable. Also, it would be stationary and so I could at least have a chance of dodging it.

Suppose instead it was a moving object. There were lots of posted signs on this mountainous road that showed the classic deer crossing symbol. If I came around a bend, and if by bad and dumb luck a deer was standing in the middle of the lane, what would I do then? The deer has a chance of moving. If I see the deer and it sees me, all happening in the same instant of time, the deer might make a choice of moving say to the right. If I had already started to steer right of the deer, I would now by on a collision path with it. So, if I had stayed straight I might have avoided it, but because it moved to the right, and because I happened to also opt to steer to the right, we now are once again going to hit each other. The boulder at least would not be playing games with me, it would just be staking out its territory and sticking with it.

Alright, I think you get the idea that when you cannot see the road ahead, you are in a perilous situation. I've indicated that once you can see the road, there might be something amiss. Each of the examples so far were of objects that were occupying the road. This led you to have to consider ways in which to do object recognition and ascertain what to do due to the object blocking your path. The object might be very large, such as the boulder, or it might be relatively smaller, such as the deer. The object might be stationary and fixed in place, or it might be an object that readily moves. The moving object might have a clear-cut trajectory, let's say the boulder was rolling down the hill and it was unlikely to change the path of the rolling, or it might have an unknown trajectory and be able to shift which way it goes, such as a deer that might go to the right and then suddenly opt to change direction and go back toward the left.

Let's make one more variation of this roadway dilemma. Suppose the roadway doesn't continue at all. Is this a Twilight Zone episode, you ask? No, really, I am serious, suppose the roadway is just not there. I could have been driving around a bend, and this was during the winter months, so the mountain itself was very wet and muddy, and suddenly not have a road left to drive on. As background for you, there had been instances of the mountain slopes deciding to slide and take out entire passages of roadway. Essentially, I could be driving directly onto and over a cliff, if the road ahead had been obliterated due to a mountain slide.

You might say that certainly there would be signs warning of this, and some kind of roadway cones or other indications that I was about to reach a gap in the roadway. Not if the slide had just happened and there was yet to be anyone that had come across the roadway. I could be the "lucky" first driver to discover that there was no more roadway ahead. There didn't need to be any warning. The roadway leading up to the curve could look perfectly fine. The roadway of the curve could be itself in pristine condition. It could be that just as you round the bend, there is a newly formed cliff. Would you be able to react in time? Would you be so shocked that you would not even be able to react and just plummet off the road?

Fortunately, I did not encounter any such breaks in the roadway. I am still alive to be able to write this sentence, thankfully.

What does this have to do with self-driving cars?

At the Cybernetic Self-Driving Car Institute, we are developing advanced AI for street scene analyses and doing what is referred to as free-space detection. This is a crucial aspect of any self-driving car and we all need to find ways to improve how it is done. The better the free-space detection, the better things will be for the safe and sound operation by the AI of the self-driving car.

Here's how free-space detection works.

The front-facing sensor cameras on the self-driving car take images of whatever is ahead of the vehicle. Those images are analyzed by the vision system to find aspects such as where is the roadway, where are objects, and the like. These findings are being done as part of the sensor fusion. The sensor fusion feeds into the AI system. The AI system receives the various roadway recognition and object recognition indications from the vision system, and updates a virtual model of the surrounding world that the self-driving car is immersed within. The AI system then needs to interpret the indicated roadway and objects to decide which direction the car should go, what speed it should go, whether the car should apply brakes, and so on.

If you are driving on an open highway, this image analysis should hopefully reveal that for example right now you have 25 feet of open roadway space between you and the car directly ahead of you. It might also have found free-space that is to your right, perhaps it is the shoulder of the highway. It might also have indicated free-space to your left, assuming you are in a two-lane road and you are in the rightmost slow lane, and there isn't a car immediately to your left and in the fast lane.

All of this free-space detection is vital to know about. If the self-driving car needs to suddenly swerve to avoid something, it needs to know if there is free-space to its left, or to its right. It needs to know how much free-space is directly ahead of it. You, as a human driver, are continually doing the same thing. Your eyes are scanning the roadway, and feeding the images to your brain. Your brain is calculating where the free-space exists. Do you have room to move up closer to the car ahead of you? Can you swing into the lane to your left? Can you go onto the shoulder of the highway if an emergency dictates doing so?

We take all of this for granted most of the time. As humans, we are well accustomed to using our vision system, our eyes, in order to look around for free-space and for objects. During driver training for novice teenage drivers, most of them will have their head pointed directly ahead and be petrified about looking anywhere but immediately ahead of the car. They are taught to be looking left and right, scanning the horizon, and be able to readily know what is around them. I've seen some student drivers that hold their head in a rigid straight ahead and manner and they are trying to get their eyeballs to shift back-and-forth, rather than moving their head back-and-forth.

Part of the reason you need to do continual scanning is because as you move the scene around you is changing. You cannot rely upon what you saw three minutes ago, that's old news. You cannot even rely on what you saw ten seconds ago. If you are driving at 65 miles per hour, you are moving forward at about 95 feet per second. This means that you need to be looking around you for free-space and be able to tell where free-space exists as you are zooming through the free-space that you moments earlier detected and decided was safe to drive through.

Imagine that you are driving on a road and you see up ahead that it is wide open. Not a car in sight. Not a boulder or deer in sight. Your eyes are seeing a lot of free-space. This lets your brain relax somewhat, because you are driving along at 95 feet per second and yet you know that there is plenty of free-space all around you. Nothing to worry about. But, suddenly, seemingly out of nowhere, a car that is going perpendicular to your road, opts to drive across your road. All of sudden, your free-space is now being occupied.

You need to now calculate mentally the path of the car that is going to cross your path. Will it continue on its path and you'll end-up going behind it, or will you pass in front of it and safely go past? Your mind also is realizing that there is free-space on the far side of that car. In other words, the car is blocking part of your view now of the road further ahead of you, but you know that there is road there, because you had seen it moments earlier, prior to the car now obstructing part of you view.

I mention this because when you are driving in a city environment, trying to visually identify free-space gets hard. There are numerous objects that can block your view. You can detect the free-space that leads up to those objects, and you can sometimes see over the object to see free-space on the other side, but part of your ability to see the free-space is being blocked visually. There might be a big truck parked on the street that is a doing a delivery and you cannot see well past the truck. There might be pedestrians walking across the street and you cannot see exactly the free-space beyond them. And so on.

For the self-driving car, this is equally an issue. It gets visual images streaming into the cameras and needs to make guesses about where the free-space exists. Even if the free-space is not shown in the image, there is a chance of free-space being there, beyond an object that is blocking part of the image that shows the roadway. As objects come and go in front of you, the system needs to keep track of where free-space is, and dynamically keep up with the changing scenery.

This is an imperfect world and so the vision system of the self-driving car is having to attach probabilities to what it is finding. Is this patch of roadway free-space or not? Rather than saying yes or no, the system might estimate that with a high probability it is free-space. Once you the car moves a few more feet, the next image flowing in might confirm the existence of the free-space, or it might lead to reducing the probability that there is free-space there due to the image analyses being done and an updated indication that there isn't free-space where the system once thought there was.

These image recognition aspects can be computationally

expensive, meaning that it takes a lot of computer processing to do. As the processors on self-driving cars get faster and less expensive, the image recognition that can be done is improved, in the sense of it can be done faster and done to a more exhaustive and detailed manner. Likewise, the cameras are getting better such that they have higher resolution and can grab sharper images and longer distance seeing images. All of this will generally improve the vision system capabilities of self-driving cars.

What has really helped too is the advent of stereo-cameras. By using stereo-cameras, the vision system on the self-driving car can gauge stereoscopic depth perception. Here's what I mean. If you look at a normal picture that you take with your smartphone, can you look at the picture and be able to know the depth of objects and the scene in the picture? Not really. You have a 2D or flat picture, and when you look at it, you need to mentally tell yourself that those people in the picture are maybe ten feet away from the camera, but how do you know? You know because of their relative size in the picture and their relative size and position in comparison to other objects in the picture. I could easily fool you by making a setting that you think involves a certain depth but I've optically fooled you.

A self-driving car is driving in a 3D world. The images from a normal camera are 2D. Yet, somehow, the self-driving car has to identify and interpret aspects of a 3D world in order to be driving safely in a 3D setting. The use of stereo-cameras allows the vision system to determine the geometry and the 3D aspects by doing various vision processing tricks, including using the stereo disparity signal. Indeed, one of the popular algorithms for doing this is the Stixel Disparity model.

Recent advances are improving how we do the vision processing. For example, by using a Fully Convolutional Network (FCN), recent efforts show that it is feasible to do self-supervised analyses of vision training sets, rather than relying upon manually annotated training sets. This allows the vision system to be more adaptive to dynamic street scenes that it has not encountered previously. It is a probabilistic framework, and uses Fourier transformation to aid in calculating the binocular disparity of locations.

I'll return to my earlier question though, namely, where is the road?

The self-driving car relies upon the vision system sensors and sensor fusion to inform it about where the road is. The road though is only being understood in a probabilities fashion. The road is there with a certain amount of confidence, or not there with a certain amount of confidence. To augment what the vision system is reporting, a good sensor fusion and AI system tries to compare with other sensory data.

If the vision system is saying that the roadway is blocked up ahead, and there is 100 feet of free-space in front of the object, and then beyond the object there is 200 feet of free-space, the AI should be asking the radar what it has found. Does the radar also detect the object that is at supposedly a position of 100 feet ahead of the existing free-space that is directly in front of the self-driving car?

This can then get tricky because suppose the vision system says there is an object at 100 feet ahead, but the radar says it detects no object up ahead. Is that because the object is beyond the range of the radar? It is because the image system has gotten optically confused by something else in the scene up ahead?

For example, one famous instance was a self-driving car that reportedly was scanning images of the scene ahead, and there was a billboard that had a car advertisement shown on the billboard, displaying pictorially a picture of a car. The image analysis system interpreted the picture of the car to be an actual car. It then conveyed to the AI system that there was a car up ahead, when in fact it was merely a picture of a car, as displayed on the billboard.

The AI system needs to be gauging whether or not the info coming from the vision system might have false positives, such as the indication that a car exists ahead when it is only a picture of a car on a billboard, or when there might be false negatives. A false negative would be when the vision system does not catch that there is an object ahead, and yet there really is an object ahead. This is also true of free-space, in that the vision system might report that there is free-space when it isn't actually there (a false positive) or report that there is no free-space when it is indeed there (a false negative).

You can imagine the dangers that loom if the AI is told or believes that free-space exists when it does not actually exist. The AI might decide to move into the next lane, since it was informed by the vision sensor that there was free-space there (meaning no object there), and then ram into a car that was in that free-space, but that the AI didn't know was there. This is similar to human drivers that don't look carefully at their side view mirrors or do but nonetheless cannot see what is in their blind spots. If they mentally believe there is nothing in their blind spot, and then make a lane change, they can ram into another car that was actually in their blind spot. By the way, I see this near-miss situation happen every morning during my early morning freeway commute.

As you can guess, the street scene analysis and detection of free-space is a cornerstone for all self-driving cars. In a dynamic manner, as the car is being driven by the AI, the sensors are feeding valuable information about where free-space exists, and where it does not exist. The AI takes this into account as it moves the vehicle from place to place. The free-space detection is especially hard in city environments. It becomes even more challenging in adverse weather conditions, such as heavy rains or snow, since the vision system is going to be partially occluded or being getting images that are slurred or smeared. The better job that the free-space detection can do, the safer the driving by the self-driving car. The poorer the job of the free-space detection, the greater the chances of the self-driving car going the wrong way, hitting objects, or driving onto space that is not viable free-space. Free-space, it's the rad thing.

CHAPTER 3

SELF-AWARENESS
FOR SELF-DRIVING CARS

CHAPTER 3

SELF-AWARENESS
FOR SELF-DRIVING CARS

You are right now reading this sentence. Your focus, presumably, involves seeing the letters on the page (or screen, if looking at this online), you can see that the letters are grouped together into words, and the words grouped into sentences, and sentences grouped into paragraphs. Your eyes are conveying the images of these characters to your brain. Your brain is analyzing the images and able somehow (we don't yet know how) to turn these images into some kind of concepts, ideas, knowledge that it then combines with other concepts, ideas, knowledge, and ultimately makes sense of what this says.

Before I pointed out that you were reading the above words, were you aware that you were reading the words?

Probably not.

You were reading the words and doing so without having to think about the fact that you were reading the words. You were just reading the words. But, if I suddenly interrupted you and asked what you are doing, you would certainly have told me that you were reading the words. We'll assume that at the time of reading the words that you actually were aware you were reading the words, since of course it could be that you weren't aware of reading the words while actually reading them and only once I asked did you then get sparked into the awareness of what you were doing.

Kind of mind numbing to walk you through this, but it's for a very good reason. As a human, you have a means to be aware of what you are doing, where you are, what you are seeing, and so on. You have self-awareness. Small children develop self-awareness over time. They at first aren't able to readily think about themselves per se. They see you and can think about you. They can look at a dog and think about the dog. It is much harder for them to think about themselves. What is Jared doing right now, you might ask a small child named Jared. Depending upon the age, the child might not comprehend that you are asking about them, and will assume you are asking about someone else named Jared, and might even look around trying to see where this Jared is.

Eventually, a child develops into realizing that they exist per se, and that they can think about their own existence. If you ask Jared what is Jared doing right now, he'll be able to use his now developed self-awareness to say that Jared is maybe playing a game on his smartphone. Once he gets a little more developed, he might be smarmy about his reply and tell you that Jared is answering your question. He now has advanced to knowing about himself and furthermore realizes he can joke with you about the aspect that though he was just playing the game that in the instant that he responds to you that he is now responding to you, rather than saying he is playing the game.

Some refer to this as knowing about knowing. We know that we know something, and we can be introspective about what we know. Do animals have this? Some experts say yes, some say no, some say that some animals have it, some say that some animals have it but only in minor ways. When you have an animal look at itself in a mirror, which seems to be a popular type of cat video on YouTube (i.e., filming your cat when it sees its own image in a mirror), the cat will often be wary of the mirrored image and even try to strike at it. This could be because it does not recognize itself, which certainly seems plausible because why would you recognize your own bodily form unless you had seen it before in a mirror, or it could be because the cat cannot mentally comprehend that it itself is a cat and is not particularly aware of its own existence (therefore, it has no recognition of what it is seeing in the mirror).

From an AI perspective, we care a lot about self-awareness.

Self-awareness seems to be an essential component of human intelligence. And, anything that is a significant component of human intelligence will most likely be needed to produce artificial intelligence. We need to understand the components that comprise human intelligence in order to produce artificial intelligence.

Well, Okay, I admit some say we don't really need to understand human intelligence directly, and can just produce machines that do what human intelligence exhibits. They believe we should untether ourselves from worrying about cracking the hidden codes and mystery of the human mind, and just go ahead and build something in a way that acts intelligently. There might be more ways than one to skin a cat (sorry about that metaphor!), in that we might be able to successfully get to artificial intelligence and bypass figuring out how humans do it.

That being said, let's get back to self-awareness. The ability to create something that is self-aware is a capability desired by those that are on the holy quest for artificial intelligence. Some call this artificial consciousness, or sometimes machine consciousness, and want to make machines that appear to have consciousness and be aware of it. It is a slippery slope since we need to define what we mean by consciousness. I am not going to be labor that whole debate. Instead, let's put it this way, go with me that being self-aware involves being aware of your own consciousness.

Let me try this from another angle. There is knowledge. Knowledge consists of the things that you know about. You know how to drive a car. You know that roads are places you can drive a car. You know that a car normally cannot fly. Etc. There is also meta-knowledge. Meta-knowledge is considered knowledge about knowledge. You are aware that you know how to drive a car. You are aware that you know that roads are places that you can drive a car. You might also be aware that you cannot drive a truck, even though you can drive a car.

Notice that your awareness allows you to know not only what you do know, but also be potentially aware of what you do not know. Suppose I ask you if you can put oil into your car. Let's suppose you say yes, you do know how to do so, since you are aware that you can put oil into your car. I ask you if you can change the oil in your car. You search your mind, you cannot find anything in it about how to change oil in a car, and so you then report to me that you do not know how to put oil into your car. You might find related info, such as that to change oil in a car you can take the car to the nearest car mechanic, and so you might say that though you don't know how to change the oil directly, you can ultimately get the oil changed by taking it to someone that does know.

There are various types of awareness. One type of awareness is to be aware of what you've done, such as being aware that you yesterday went to the store and bought a can of peas. Another is to be aware of what you are planning to do. You might be aware that you have a goal of driving your car to the beach later this afternoon. Another form of awareness is about your body and your sensors. You are aware that your ears are not working very well at this moment because you just got out of the swimming pool and your eyes are still filled with water. Various debates exist among researchers about how many types of awareness there are. Some say it is a finite number of types and call them such aspects as agency awareness, sensorimotor awareness, goal awareness, and so on. Some argue that there are tons of different kinds of awareness.

A few AI researchers have boldly proclaimed (some say recklessly and loosely) that they somehow have created self-awareness in robots. There is one well known example of a researcher that claims he developed a robot that can recognize itself in a mirror. This is similar to my comment earlier about the cat and whether it can recognize itself in a mirror. Robots right now that seemingly recognize their mirrored image are criticized by some as a bit of a cheap trick and not truly representative of the kind of self-awareness that we speak of when referring to human self-awareness.

Why does this have anything to do with self-driving cars?

At the Cybernetic Self-Driving Car Institute, we believe that self-awareness for a self-driving car is essential for ultimately reaching a true Level 5 self-driving car.

Let's take a look at what it means for a self-driving car to have self-awareness.

Today, a self-driving car will readily drive you along a freeway road and watch for things like cars ahead of you that might be slowing or stopping, or be looking for lane markers that suddenly shift direction and so the self-driving car needs to also shift direction. This is akin to the small child that can play a game on their smartphone, it is an act of doing something that they have an ability to undertake. Is though the self-driving car "aware" that it is in fact driving you along on the freeway? Is it aware that it is looking for the lane markers? Or, is it just carrying out the required actions and not in any sense aware that it is doing so?

At the most strategic level of the AI of a self-driving car, we posit that the topmost layer of AI must be doing self-awareness types of activities. The topmost layer should be observing its own behavior, and figuring out what the significance of that behavior is. It is an omnipresent overseer of itself. This is what we are suggesting be considered self-awareness in the case of self-driving cars.

I'll freely state that this does not in any manner whatsoever indicate or imply that the AI must be conscious. We are merely borrowing the valuable aspects of self-awareness as it is understood to exist in humans and making sure that we embody that into the AI of the self-driving car.

Why would this make a difference? It will allow a self-driving car to do a much better job at driving a self-driving car. Maybe getting us that much closer to the Level 5 true self-driving car. By being aware of its own efforts, the self-driving car should do whatever any sentient being would presumably do, namely use the self-awareness to improve itself, improve whatever it is doing right now, improve what it will be doing next, and otherwise seeking safety and well-being for itself.

A self-driving car is driving along and detects that traffic up ahead has come to a halt. The AI has one kind of awareness that the self-driving car is going 50 miles per hour and headed straight into the stopped cars ahead. It attempts to calculate stopping distances and figure out what to do. As it is figuring out what to do, the car is still rolling forward at 50 mph. The self-driving car needs to be self-aware that it is taking time to determine what to do, and during that time it is getting itself into further hot water. Maybe it should therefore abandon the detailed time consuming analysis of what to do and pick instead a quick standby recourse that is ready for whenever needed. Or, maybe it should seek out assistance from other connected cars about what to do.

The self-awareness also applies to what the self-driving car itself can and cannot do. Just as I mentioned earlier that self-awareness encompasses things you know and also knowing if you don't know something, likewise for the self-driving car. Suppose the guts of the self-driving car come back about this problem of what to do about the stopped cars ahead, and it recommends that the self-driving car immediately jam on the brakes. Is this the right solution?

Suppose the self-awareness element knows that the self-driving car has been having brake related issues lately. The brakes are not available at their usual capability. This is something that needs to be considered when determining the viability of slamming on the brakes. Furthermore, suppose the self-awareness knows that the occupants of the car are not wearing their seat belts. If the self-driving car proceeds to slam on the brakes, the occupants will go flying around the innards of the car and potentially get injured.

The topmost AI layer using this self-awareness opts to nix the proposed tactic of slamming on the brakes. Instead, it recommends that the self-driving car swerve to the left and go into the carpool lane. Now, it could be that the self-driving car doesn't have enough occupants to legally go into the carpool lane, but the self-awareness figures that it will be worthwhile as a gambit to save the occupants from injury or death, and if this means getting a traffic ticket it is worth it to do so.

All of this kind of reasoning needs to be included into the AI of the self-driving car. It is the strategic level "thinking" that will get us toward cars that can drive as humans can. Humans are self-aware of what they are doing as they drive. At the moment of doing something, a human might not be aware of the awareness, but when prompted the human will either register what they are doing or possibly playback mentally what they were doing. Self-aware by a self-driving car should be taking place at all times, and then especially invoked when the circumstances warrant.

This is a very practical aspect of AI for self-driving cars.

Now, I know that some of you will try to take this to the extreme. If the self-driving car can be self-aware, does this take us down the path that it will soon be able to start making its own decisions? You might be aware that the famous computer scientist and mathematician John von Neumann indicated in the 1950s that someday AI systems might reach a point of what he coined singularity. Singularity is an idea that AI will become conscious and realize that it exists, and this might then trigger the AI to want to take over mankind. A runaway reaction of one AI combining forces with other AI's might allow the AI to gang up on us humans.

I certainly enjoy watching science fiction movies depicting this aspect, but we aren't anywhere close to that today. I think we are safe right now to try and leverage self-awareness aspects in our AI for self-driving cars. Of course, I could be saying this only because an AI system is pointing a laser at my head and threatening me if I don't say that it is Okay to let AI systems become self-aware.

.

.

CHAPTER 4
CARTOGRAPHIC
TRADE-OFFS
FOR SELF-DRIVING CARS

CHAPTER 4

CARTOGRAPHIC TRADE-OFFS FOR SELF-DRIVING CARS

I was driving in an area of Beverly Hills that has some of the priciest retail establishments in the world, and then went up to a mansion in nearby Beverly Glen for a special VIP party. The Beverly Glen area is one that I have rarely driven into. No problem, I figured, since I could use the GPS on my smartphone to guide me around. I entered the destination address into my smartphone and away I went. As I entered into the tony Beverly Glen neighborhoods, there were massive homes with equally massive iron gates surrounding their properties. It was also very lush, including quite a number of trees to help further hide and protect the homes from the prying eyes of others.

The hills there tend to rise and fall, and upon slowly making my way around the curved hilly sides I began to realize that I no longer was getting a signal on my smartphone. Apparently, this was presumably another desired protection by the well to do homeowners. Keep away strangers by not having any cell connection in the area. I found out later on that the homeowners all pretty much rely upon their cable and satellite providers for cell coverage in their homes and across their properties. The party I attended had about 15 wireless access points distributed all around the property.

Anyway, I found myself trying to find the party but my GPS wasn't able to get updated. I was lost! In the olden days, I would have grabbed up my trusty Thomas Guide. Those of you that don't know, it was the golden map provider for anywhere you might want to go. You'd keep various Thomas Guide maps in your car, such as maps of Los Angeles,

Orange County, San Diego, Santa Barbara, San Francisco, all places in California you might be heading to. If you were driving out of town, you'd get yourself Thomas Guide maps for wherever you might be going. The backseat of my car had tons of those maps. Of course, now, we just rely upon our electronic GPS.

Question for you. Without my GPS, would I be unable to drive my car? I hope you would say that no, I wasn't somehow prevented from driving my car. Obviously, you say, I was certainly able to drive my car. I was just though driving without necessarily knowing how to get to where I wanted to go. I could still drive. The car was still able to move along on the roads. I could look at street signs and see the names of streets. It might take a bit longer to find my way, but yes, I could drive and I could proceed.

Does this elicit a ho-hum from you? It might. You would likely think that I was stating the obvious. As a human driver, and having a working car, I could still drive around, even though I had no map. The lack of a map did not stop me from wandering around. The reason that this is an important point is because I am about to discuss self-driving cars. Ready?

Today, some are saying that any self-driving car that doesn't have maps is unable to drive. In other words, no maps, no driving. This is because some of the self-driving car makers are tying the use of a map into whatever the self-driving car tries to do while driving. If you want the self-driving car to take you on a trip to Disneyland, it needs maps to know which streets to take. It needs to route via the maps and determine when to make a left turn, when to make a right turn, and so on. Without a map, the self-driving car is useless.

At the Cybernetic Self-Driving Car Institute, we don't believe that a lack of having a map is a nonstarter for a self-driving car. We make the assumption that there might be times that the self-driving car does not have a map available. In which case, the self-driving should still be able to drive.

Yikes, you say, a blind self-driving car that is going on the roads and doesn't know where it is going, this sounds like a recipe for disaster.

Keep in mind that the self-driving car should still be able to drive on the roads and be able to do things like stopping at lighted intersections and making left turns and right turns. These should be based on whatever the self-driving car encounters when it encounters it.

Similar to my story above about driving around Beverly Glen, I was able to drive up and down the streets even without having a map. It would have been much easier to get to my destination if I had a map, but I wasn't stuck and unable to move. Having a fundamental understanding of how to drive a car, and following the flow of the streets, making legal turns, and otherwise just driving on the roads, I could get around. In this case, I also had the street signs on the corners of the streets, which I then was able to read and determine what street I was on.

Believe it or not, I even made a quickly hand drawn diagram of my own, a map if you were. I became suddenly a cartographer. As an amateur cartographer, I penciled out the neighborhood by making lines for the roads and created a small grid on a piece of paper. I labeled the streets based on the street signs. I noted some landmarks along the way, such as a house with a large letter P emblazoned on its roof (the ponderosa?), and I also saw a nifty koi pond at the front of one house (made a mental note to go back there one day and see the koi fish).

If I had been really doing a good job and uses my skills as a former Scout Master for my son's Boy Scout Troop, I would have added topographical markings to my budding map. I could have guessed at the elevations. I could have marked whether the road was tending up or tending downward. Other aspects of the terrain could have been noted. But, in this case, I just wanted to get to the party. That was more important than making a cool map.

In the news lately about self-driving cars there are some complaining that China is not letting foreign companies go into China and make electronic maps of the roadways there. Some self-driving car makers outside of China are saying that without being able to make maps, their self-driving cars won't be usable in China. This seems a bit overblown. The self-driving cars will be usable, but admittedly not as effective. No doubt about that.

Also, I can guess that Chinese companies that are allowed to create maps will then be able to charge exorbitant prices to the self-driving car makers that want to have their cars driving in China. Sure, that's a problem. This also seems to be forcing non-Chinese map making firms to have to buddy up to Chinese mapping firms. It's a socio-political issue, and it does then impact self-driving cars in terms of the added costs.

Some self-driving car makers insist that without maps, the self-driving car won't be able to provide as smooth a ride. Their claim is that by examining a map beforehand, the AI can ascertain which roads are bad and which are good. If a road is bad, meaning all torn up and poorly maintained, the self-driving car will bounce around during that part of the trip. The occupants of the self-driving car will get a jostled ride. If the a road is good, meaning in quality shape and smooth, it will help the self-driving car to provide a non-jarring ride. That all makes sense and I appreciate that the self-driving car makers want to use whatever they can to ensure that the self-driving car operates well and that the occupants are treated to as smooth a ride as possible.

Where do maps come from?

We are used to the satellite maps that you can get online. For those, the self-driving cars can use them to plan out overall aspects of a trip, but it is often not detailed enough to get down to the specific street aspects (we're getting there). A self-driving car could either store the satellite generated maps in the memory of the car, or it could use a communication connection to access such maps. The downside of the communication connection approach involves circumstance like I experienced whereby there was not a communication connection available.

The problem with storing maps in the memory of the self-driving car is that the maps might be outdated in comparison to what might be online. From a design perspective for a self-driving car, it is best to use both methods in conjunction with each other. Store maps on-board the self-driving car, and augment those maps with the communication connection when available.

The maps are often provided by the car maker. The car maker usually though didn't create the maps, they bought them or licensed them from someone else that made the maps. A major map provider might have detailed maps generally, but often might not have localized maps. Third parties that make localized maps often then provide that last mile of detailed indications.

Another approach involves crowdsourcing for a map. There are companies that actually will pay people to help make local maps. You might have heard that Apple is desperate to get its maps used over say Google Maps, and has indicated that freelancers that want to earn some extra cash can do so for a small payment to them for each map addition or confirmation they make. Yes, you could earn a fortune helping to make maps, get going today!

Should a self-driving car believe a map? We say a self-driving car should use a mode of trust but verify. Just because a map says one thing, it does not mean that the actual road will be what the maps says. I was in San Diego last month, and after doing some work there, I wanted to get back to the major freeway and make my way home. I mapped using my in-car GPS. I dutifully followed its instructions. The voice told me to make a turn here, go straight a quarter mile, make another turn, and so on. I eventually could see that I was almost to the freeway. Upon one of the last instructions before I would get to the freeway onramp, I took the turn that the GPS said to do, and suddenly found myself at a dead-end. The road came to a dead-end. The GPS map showed that the road continued to the freeway entrance. I could see the freeway entrance, and I am betting that at some point the road did go through, but not anymore.

The point is that the self-driving car should be using its sensors to verify that what the maps says is true and accurate. The map provides overall guidance, but it should not be used to blindly drive the car into whatever trap awaits. The AI has to assume that for whatever reason there is a chance that the map being used will be faulty. It might be outdated. It might be inaccurate.

A map could even be intentionally falsified. Here's an example of what some critics of self-driving cars are concerned about. You are a wealthy person, or maybe a known celebrity or political figure. You get into your true self-driving car, assume that it is a Level 5. You settle into the self-driving car, have a few drinks, relax, and don't pay attention to the driving journey. There isn't any reason to pay attention since you aren't the driver. You are merely a passenger along for the ride to your desired destination. Leave the driving to the AI.

Suppose someone has hacked the maps that you are using. You have indicated to the self-driving car where you want to go, doing via in-car commands. The hacked maps fool the AI system into taking a particular route that appears to go to the desired destination. In fact, what has happened is that kidnappers are waiting at a point of the trip that they know the self-driving car will come to. Once the self-driving car arrives there, they will take the occupants and kidnap them, and maybe even take the car too.

This is a valid concern.

There are some ways to try and prevent or at least reduce the chances of this. For example, if the AI has multiple maps, it could compare the routes to see whether one is suspicious in comparison to the others. There also could be special encryption coding in the maps so that if they are hacked it would reveal that something amiss has happened to the map. Most self-driving car makers are assuming that the map they are using is perfectly fine and clean. They aren't resorting to encryption or other protective measures, and they aren't dealing with any redundancy and double-checking. This might seem like an overkill measure now, but once we have lots of self-driving cars on the roadway, and a few instances of map tampering, I am betting there will be a scramble by the self-driving car makers to do something about it.

Let's assume that at some point while in your self-driving car, it cannot access maps or otherwise there just aren't any maps for where you are. What should the self-driving car do?

It could use commonly known maze traversal techniques to make its way.

We have made use of the simple random mouse algorithm for a self-driving car that otherwise does not have a map available. This approach involves making random choices at junctions and is based on a constrained maze. It can work to some degree when in a neighborhood like the Beverly Glen example I mentioned before. This is augmented by the self-driving car vision system that is looking for the street signs that say the name of the street.

Another maze traversal technique is Tremaux's algorithm. This is akin to how I made my own map while driving around Beverly Glen. The AI essentially creates a map as it goes along. The paths taken are then marked. There are other recursive algorithms that can also be used. All of these need to be considered in light of where the self-driving car is trying to drive. A classic maze shape might not be a proper fit to the locale of the driving journey.

In recap, a self-driving car should be doing this:

- Use a map if available
- Store the map on-board
- Augment with external maps via communication
- Trust but verify the map as the driving journey proceeds
- Be on alert for maps that are outdated, inaccurate, etc.
- Protect and detect for falsified maps
- Use multiple maps to do double-checks
- Be able to drive on a journey even when maps aren't available
- Use various maze traversal techniques and create a map as warranted
- Potentially interact with the occupants as needed

No map does not mean no trip. Self-driving cars don't need to be grounded simply because of a lack of an available map. Eventually, with V2V (vehicle-to-vehicle communication), a self-driving car that lacks a map might be able to bum a map off another vehicle (if it makes sense and is safe to do so). Crowdsourcing of maps is predicted to occur by self-driving cars that learn from each other. That's a ways off in the future, and so meanwhile it still makes sense to have a self-driving car that can drive without a map and make its own map. Adapt and overcome.

CHAPTER 5

TOLL ROAD TRAVERSAL
FOR
SELF-DRIVING CARS

CHAPTER 5

TOLL ROAD TRAVERSAL
FOR SELF-DRIVING CARS

Toll roads, love them or hate them.

For many years, the west coast of the United States was proud to say that toll roads were verboten. Sure, there might be one here or there, but otherwise the west coasters believed that the prevalence of toll roads on the east coast was abysmal. Over my dead body would we have toll roads, exclaimed many drivers in the Los Angeles and surrounding areas. Barbaric, was the apt description for toll roads. This was California, the land that made the word "freeway" come to popularity and did so because it was indeed a "free way."

No more.

With complaints about clogged freeways and rising commute times, the toll road concept began to become a tolerated topic. At first, tolls were reserved for special circumstances like a bridge crossing. Even there, it was initially a toll in both directions, but the cries of foul were so large that things were changed to charge a toll in just one direction. Then, some brand new freeways were built and for those the notion of having a toll was introduced. This seemed to make sense.

Rather than upset the status quo and put a toll on an existing freeway, one that was considered free, instead plop a toll onto a new freeway. There weren't any traditions on the use of the new freeway.

Starting it with a toll established a new tradition for that particular freeway. It also seemed sensible to the general public since they assumed that the cost to build the new freeway had to be covered somehow and a toll was the reasonable way to do so.

Whichever way you cut it, toll roads are now everywhere, east coast by tradition and west coast by more recent adoption. In this modern age, I know that you are thinking that handling a toll is pretty easy. Just get the cars to have some kind of transponder and when the car drives up to a toll position, the toll system can register the transponder and charge the person for their use of the toll road. No need to slow down or stop the car. No need to dig in the car for loose change to pay for the toll. No need to carry on conversation with a toll taker that has nothing to do other than take tolls, give change, and talk about the weather.

Well, we aren't yet living in a world with transponders on every car. As a result, most of the toll roads still need to have a means to let toll payment occur via cash. On some toll roads, they charge you as you exit the toll road. At the exit position are buckets that you place cash into. The bucket collects the cash, counts it, and then either opens a gate or flashes a signal to say you've paid. If you try to skip or cheat it, the system takes a photo of you and your license plate. The next thing you know, there's a ticket being mailed to you, or at least to the registered owner of the car.

For entry into a toll road, most still have a human toll taker. The human stands in a guard shack. A car drives up to the guard shack. The driver hands cash to the toll taker. The toll taker receives the cash, counts it, and provides back any needed change. The toll taker then either opens a gate, or sets a signal that lights up to say that you can proceed. The toll taker is supposed to work fast. Cars are supposed to be ready to make payment. It should all happen in an orderly manner. Efficient payment and green lighting of cars to move ahead onto the toll road.

The reality is that often there is utter chaos at the toll gates. Especially you see turmoil during rush hour. You've got cars driven by drivers that aren't familiar with the terrain and the toll gate, and so they don't know which lane to get into. There are some lanes reserved for transponder payers, other lanes for cash only, and some lanes for both cash and transponder. When I went across the Oakland Bay Bridge the other day, I noticed that another part of the confusion was how much the toll was. There were numerous signs and each was like one of those contracts that has small print and you need to be a lawyer to figure out what to do.

In the case of the Oakland Bay Bridge, the signs said the price was $6 if it was a weekday between certain daytime hours, or $5 if it was other hours during the daytime, and $4 if it was weekends but only with some added provisions. There were other signs about the number of axles on the vehicle and how much you needed to pay per axle. I could see some of the drivers being quite perplexed and unable to figure out beforehand how much the cost would be. They tended to just hand over a ten-dollar bill to the toll taker and hope that the toll taker would be honest and return the right amount of change for the actual toll required.

Why all this discussion about toll roads?

It's because a self-driving car has to contend with toll roads. For a true self-driving car, which I define as a Level 5, the self-driving car should be able to figure out what to do. The main aspect to figure out is usually the entry point and the exit point. Once a self-driving car is actually on the toll road, the road is about the same as any other road. There's nothing particularly special about the toll road itself. Just more asphalt and it cost you a few bucks to have the privilege to drive on it.

At the Cybernetic Self-Driving Car Institute, we are developing AI software that aids the self-driving car in terms of traversal during the entry into the toll road and the exit from the toll road. This is a kind of "edge problem" for self-driving cars, meaning it is not a core aspect, it only comes up on occasion, but that it is something that ultimately a self-driving car needs to be able solve and carry out.

Let's walk through the fundamentals of how the AI system handles the toll road situation.

Using maps, the AI would already be likely aware that a toll entry is coming up. That being the case, it could also let the occupant of the self-driving car know that a toll is nearing. The occupant could decide to try and have the self-driving car navigate a different path to avoid dealing with the toll and the toll road. You've likely seen this option on your existing GPS system. The GPS will let you know that the path requires a toll, and you can select an alternative path if you wish. This interaction with the occupants of a self-driving car would be undertaken via in-car commands.

Suppose the AI system doesn't have a map, or has a map that is faulty or outdated and does not indicate that a toll road is ahead. In which case, the AI system has to detect that a toll road is upcoming, doing so without the use of a map. One way to detect a toll road is upcoming would be by reading the road signs that usually precede a toll road.

When the self-driving car gets near to the entrance of the toll road, this is usually where the heavy lifting takes place. There is going to be a lot of stimuli that needs to be collected, analyzed, and used to make crucial and real-time decisions.

In the model of a toll entrance with toll guard shacks and multiple lanes, which is a prevalent enough model to warrant its own AI capability, the self-driving car needs to collect the radar, LIDAR, camera data and figure out that there are guard shacks, there are lanes, there are signs about what to do. The AI system examines the images from the camera to ascertain which lane has which purpose. Changing lanes in this situation can be dicey.

I say this because you've got to keep in mind that the self-driving car is going to be mixing with human driven cars. Human drivers are notorious for rapid lane changes in these situations. They also tend to get really close to other cars. They tend to be rude to other cars. They tend to play chicken with other cars. It's a cruel world there at the entrance to the gates of the toll road.

There are some self-driving car makers that are saying that the toll road problem is not a problem, simply because they will hand the driving over to a human driver in the car, and let that human driver deal with the few minutes involved in traversal at the toll gate entrance. This might be OK for the levels less than a 5, but it is not allowed for a Level 5. A level 5 car is supposed to be able to be driven by the AI in whatever manner a human could drive the car. In this case, a human could traverse the entrance area, and thus so should a Level 5 self-driving car.

Another reason that some self-driving car makers claim this is a non-problem is by saying that any self-respecting self-driving car will already have a transponder or at least some method of doing the automatic payment for the toll. First, I disagree that it is axiomatic that all self-driving cars will be equipped with a transponder for the paying of tolls. Even if it came with a transponder, there are numerous different kinds of transponders and one that works for toll roads in say Los Angeles does not necessarily work for paying tolls in San Francisco. Until we have an across-the-board standard transponder for all toll roads everywhere, you are out of luck about thinking that the self-driving car will be able to simply have a universal transponder in it.

Of course, instead of a transponder, it could be that a self-driving car might have other means to deal with paying the toll. For example, if the self-driving car has some kind of electronic communication capability such as using the Internet, it could presumably pay the toll via electronic means. Once again though, the electronic communication needs to be pre-established and if you are driving across the country, and maybe you setup some means to pay electronically in California, but you are now in Arizona, the electronic communication might not do you any good there.

Even if you magically had either a transponder or some other electronic communications, the self-driving car still needs to figure out which lane to use. I used to think that all toll gates had the transponders lanes to the left and the cash lanes to the right. I've since then discovered that it seems much more randomly arranged. I've seen it all. There have been transponder lanes to the right, and cash lanes to the left. There are truck-only lanes and car-only lanes. There are mixed lanes that allow both transponders and cash, and sometimes are truck-only or car-only, or are for both trucks and cars. It's a free-for-all.

So, the self-driving car needs to scan for roadway signs about how to handle the toll road entry. Interpreting these signs can be tricky. As I said earlier, it can be tricky for humans, and so it is likely then also tricky for the AI. There is also not an obvious indication by simply inspecting the line-up of the vehicles. In other words, you could detect that trucks are all in one lane, and deduce that it probably is a truck-only lane. Thus, at least you could eliminate that lane for a self-driving car. Trying to ascertain whether the cars ahead of you have a transponder or not, there's no clear cut visual clue. It used to be that a transponder was bulky and at times visible to the naked eye. Nowadays they are much subtler and often hidden on a car.

Another approach to figuring out the right lane would be to do V2V (vehicle-to-vehicle communication). Your self-driving car could communicate with a fellow self-driving car that is nearby. It might ask the other self-driving car as to which lane should be used. The other self-driving car might know, perhaps it has used this toll road before and "learned" how to traverse it. The V2V would allow the learned self-driving car to bring the other self-driving car up-to-speed about what to do at the toll entrance. We are still pretty far from having V2V, and certainly not on any widespread basis, so this is a low odds approach currently.

You might say that another approach would be to "learn" from crowdsourcing. By this, I mean that the self-driving car might be connected via electronic communication with a server being maintained by the self-driving car maker. The server might be a collective wisdom from all of the self-driving cars that the car maker has put onto the road. The self-driving car approaching the toll road could inquire of the collective data on the server as to what to do when it gets to the toll road. This though requires that an electronic communication be available, and that the server would actually have something useful to say about traversing the toll road. Another low odds approach currently.

Looks like we'll need to use brute force. The AI will have to figure out by the signage and by the behavior of other vehicles as to which lane to get into. It needs to then moderate the speed of the self-driving car as appropriate for the toll gate entrance configuration. Usually, you tone down your speed as you get close to the toll shack. You then come to a complete stop at the toll shack.

At this point, the self-driving car has presumably alerted the human occupant that a toll needs to be paid. The self-driving car has positioned the car at a place that would allow for payment. The human in the toll shack could have already been imaged scanned and the self-driving car can do a pretty good job of lining up the car window to where the human is, allowing the human occupant to readily reach out and provide the needed cash.

I know that it might seem silly that we've had all this AI figure out where to place the self-driving car so that then a human can pay the other human some cash. Those of you that abhor the use of human labor when automation can suffice, will certainly be disturbed that this last step involves a human to human transaction. All I can say is that I agree that eventually this will no longer be the case. We should ultimately have it all be electronic.

A smarmy person might say that we should develop a robotic arm that could reach out of the car and pay the cash toll. An even smarmier person could say that we should develop a robot arm for the toll taker. You'd then have one robot arm that hands over cash to another robot arm. This, you have to admit, is even more beguiling than the scenario of one human arm reaching out to pay to another human arm. One would think that if we went to the trouble to use robotics arms, it would by then be the case that no cash needed to be physically exchanged and it would be all electronically handled.

Assuming that the cash payment is made, the AI then would detect that the gate is opened or that a green light or something has signaled that the self-driving car can proceed. At this juncture, the self-driving car can switch into a more traditional driving mode, since we are now getting into the toll road and as I said before this part is pretty routine.

The only twist though is that often when a car first passes past the toll gate, other cars are doing likewise. This can create a crazy situation of cars trying to accelerate rapidly and also do wild lane changes. You've probably seen this before. It is as though human drivers think they are at a Nascar race and that someone has shot-off the starter gun to get going. The self-driving car needs to realize that this is a common aspect and be wary of other cars that might tend to threaten the self-driving car. By threatening, I mean that the other cars might be very aggressively driven and cut-off the self-driving car.

The exit situation is generally similar. The AI needs to be looking for signage about whether a payment is needed at the exit point. The self-driving car needs to detect the exit point and scan for the payment location, if there is one. The AI needs to alert the human occupant about an upcoming payment. The self-driving car then needs to come to a stop at whatever placement is appropriate. The human occupant pays and the self-driving car needs to detect that payment was made and that it now okay for the self-driving car to proceed.

I have one suggestion for everyone. Get rid of tolls, and we'd not need to have self-driving cars that knew how to traverse the entrance and exits of toll roads.

Now, I realize that some will complain at me and say that tolls aren't the problem. It's what we do with the money. It's that the money is needed to fund our transportation infrastructure. Yes, I get it. Didn't mean to start a whole sociopolitical debate.

Meanwhile, this is an interesting edge problem for self-driving cars. It not only solves an actual driving problem, it also showcases how subtle the human driving task can be, and yet so complex, namely, the act of traversing a toll gate for entering and exiting a toll road takes a lot more "intelligence" than it might seem at first glance. Watch any novice teenage driver try to do this for the first time, and you'll witness first-hand how difficult it can be. Anyway, can I say down-with-tolls, or will that make some readers get upset at me?

CHAPTER 6

PREDICTIVE SCENARIO MODELING FOR SELF-DRIVING CARS

CHAPTER 6

PREDICTIVE SCENARIO MODELING FOR SELF-DRIVING CARS

I see the future.

Do you see the future?

Humans seem to have a relatively unique cognitively ability to envision the future. We make predictions about what will happen in the future. Sometimes, the predictions are perhaps relatively obvious, such as if you see a coffee mug teetering on your office desk that you might make a prediction it will fall off the desk, hit the floor, shatter, and the coffee will spill. Pretty much any of us can make that kind of a prediction and "foresee" the future. Young children at first aren't very good at such predictions and even the coffee example might be a surprise to them as it seemingly suddenly tumbles off the desk. They learn though about existing events and circumstances and how to extend those events and circumstances into the future.

More complex predictions though begin to stretch out our cognitive abilities. Let's suppose you are planning for a dinner party. You make arrangements to use a beautiful outdoor venue. The barbeque is setup, burgers and hot dogs purchased, buckets of ice are obtained, party hats are purchased, outdoor lights are obtained, you even buy some outdoor speakers to ensure that music will accompany the event.

So far, you are doing all this as based on a plan. The plan is shaped around a future event. You are desirous of having a dinner party at some point in the future. It is not taking place this instant and instead it is going to occur in the future. Someone exterior to all of this and that is looking at you going to the store to buy food, get ice, and doing all these other aspects might be confused because you don't seem to be consuming them at the moment you get them. You are hoarding these items. For what purpose?

If you were to thoughtfully review the clues, such as the hot dogs and burgers purchased, the fact that party hats were obtained, and so on, you could likely figure out that this person is planning a dinner party. This seems to be an apt prediction. Do you know with absolute certainty that's what is going to take place? No, you don't. Maybe it is a lunch time party, or maybe the person is going to give away these items to someone else and there isn't a single event taking place. There could be lots of other scenarios about where this is all heading. Generally, I think we would all agree that it though seems like pretty strong odds that the effort is aimed toward a future dinner party.

I mentioned earlier that predictions and seeing the future seem to be relatively unique to humans. There have been some research studies that suggest we are not alone on this planet in terms of being able to see the future. A recent study by Swedish researchers Can Kabadayi and Mathias Osvath provides some fascinating insights into ravens. You might find of interest that the he two animals we most believe have some kind of predictive capabilities are apes and ravens. Apes and ravens continue to be popular subjects of various scientific cognition experiments, hoping to determine whether or not those animals really can-do predictions and planning for the future.

Why should anyone care if animals can do this? If there are animals that can do so, it helps us to better understand what takes place when we all are in the midst of making predictions and seeing the future. Besides studying how it is done in terms of behavior, we could also be mapping the brains and try to see if we can ascertain where and how the brain does this. If we can map the brain to find where the brain does this, we have a heightened chance of mimicking the brain via say artificial neural networks to see if we can get the same kind of behavior to arise.

I suppose a more cynical person might say we want to know more about apes and raven's abilities to predict the future because we are worried about them one day taking over earth from us humans. Maybe it will be called the planet of the apes and ravens.

Anyway, for the recent study on ravens, here's what the Swedish researchers had to say: "Human planning is often characterized by decisions about future events that will unfold at other locations. The cognitive skill set that allows for planning outside the current sensory context operates across a range of domains, from planning a dinner party to making retirement plans. Such decisions require a host of cognitive skills, including mental representation of a temporally distant event, the ability to outcompete current sensorial input in favor of an unobservable goal, and understanding which current actions lead to the achievement of the delayed goal."

I would like to highlight some aspects of what they laid out. Predictions about the future and planning for that envisioned future do involve fascinating and crucial cognitive skills. You need to have some kind of mental model about a future event, taking place off in the future, so it is considered to be a time displaced temporally distant event. You need to overcome your existing sensory inputs such as your eyes and your ears, and not process the input coming in at that moment per se, and instead outcompete or focus on unobservable goals rather than immediate goals. We normally expect an animal to simply see or hear what it sees or hears at the moment and take immediate action. A willingness to delay taking action, and anticipate a future event, that is not so easy a task to do.

You also need to line-up current actions and do so as part of preparation for that future and currently unobservable goal. As the researches emphasized: "Well-developed self-control is essential to planning because impulsivity keeps one stuck in the immediate context." If you were to allow yourself to constantly react to immediate stimuli, you would get mired in the present and never be able to prepare for and then cope with the future. If you watch a small child, you'll see this kind of behavior. Daddy, I want some ice cream. Not now, it will spoil your dinner. I want it now. I want it now! We all know it today as so-called instant gratification. Don't put off today what you can instantly do, just be in a reactive mode. The problem with always being in a reactive mode is that you are going to likely get walloped by the future and not be ready for it.

For the dinner party, suppose that after all that planning, and after doing the setup, it turns out that on the day of that dinner party the weather turns foul and heavy rains pour down. Yikes, one ruined outdoor party. The prediction of the future envisioned nice weather, but the reality turned out to be ugly weather. Could this also have been predicted? Yes, it could have. Again, you might not have known with a certainty that it would get ugly, but you could have anticipated that it might, and thus, taken additional precautions.

What does this have to do with self-driving cars?

I am glad you asked.

At the Cybernetic Self-Driving Car Institute, we are enhancing the ability of AI to do predictive scenario modeling for self-driving cars. This consists of having the AI create various future scenarios based on current activities and states of the self-driving car, and identify future states that then can allow for the appropriate planning and carrying out of driving journey plans.

The other day, I was on the highway and driving around 65 miles per hour (I might have been going faster, but I refuse to confess here and maybe get a speeding ticket in a Minority Report movie kind of way). Anyway, if you are going at 65 mph, this means you are doing about 95 feet per second. Every second of time, you are traveling nearly 100 feet in distance. The average car length is about 15 feet. This means that if you are allowing let's say two to three car lengths between you and the car ahead of you, you are giving yourself a cushion of about 30 to 45 feet in case you need to come to a sudden stop. The problem though is that at a pace of going 100 feet per second, and if you include a delay in your reaction time to hit the brakes, which experiments suggest it takes at least 5-7 seconds for you to react, you'll most likely ram into the car ahead of you if it has jammed on its brakes. Just wanted to let you know.

I was watching the traffic around and trying to be a good driver. As a good driver, you are supposed to be aware of the surrounding traffic and the roadway conditions, doing so at all times. You need to be alert and ready to react. If you are trying to watch a video that is playing on the central console of your car, or trying to tap a text message into your smartphone, you are not being alert and ready to react. I am pointing my accusing finger at some of you. Just saying.

I was behind a car. The car was doing the speed of traffic. I could have just regulated my own driving based on the car ahead of me. I like to think more broadly, so I was looking ahead of the car ahead of me. Let's call the car directly ahead of me as car number 1, or C1. The car ahead of C1 will be number C2. And so on. This will make things easier for me to tell my story.

I was keeping a proper distance between me and C1. C1 was keeping at most one to two car lengths from C2. This is insufficient stopping distance. C2 was keeping almost no distance between it and C3, essentially C2 was riding the bumper of C3. This is a classic driving suicide position. C4 was ahead of C3 by about four car lengths. We're all going around 65 miles per hour. The scenario right now is that we have me, C1, C2, C3, C4. We are all logically interconnected for a moment in time because we are on the same road, traveling in the same direction, going at roughly the same speed, and acting like a "pack" of cars, even though none of us knows each other and have never met before.

It seemed to me that C1 was focusing solely on C2, and C2 was focusing solely on C3, and C3 was focusing solely on C4. I don't know this to be a fact. It just seemed that way. I was watching all of them to be wary in case anyone in this chain of cars might sputter or do something untoward. I then noticed that C4, the car that is at the head of this pack, began to make a sudden swerve to the right. I could see their car do this, and it caught my immediate attention. Since it was a few car lengths ahead of C3, I instantly watched to see whether C3 was going to make a similar maneuver or not.

I was mentally making a prediction that perhaps there was some roadway debris up ahead. C4 was the first to encounter the roadway debris, due to being at the head of the pack. Its swerve was an early sign that something was amiss, and the debris prediction seemed plausible. If C3 also swerved, it would tend to confirm the scenario that C4 had swerved due to debris. I could then also predict that C2 would ultimately swerve. I could also predict that C1 would likely swerve. I also wondered whether any of this cascading swerving might produce other adverse consequences. Maybe instead of swerving, a panic by say driver in C2 might have him or her hit their brakes, rather than swerving or in addition to swerving.

The aspect that C4 swerved to the right was another clue. Perhaps the debris, assuming it was a debris related situation, might be at the far left of the lane. This would likely have the driver of C4 opt to swerve to the right, avoiding the debris. If the debris were in the right side of the lane, it seems likely that the C4 would have swerved to the left, entering into the fast lane, momentarily, in order to avoid the debris. A swerve to the right seemed to suggest that there was debris up ahead, and it was sitting toward the left side of this lane.

Of course, there could be lot of other explanations. Maybe the driver of C4 has a bee in their car and they are trying to swat the bee and so happened to swerve to the right. Maybe the driver of C4 was watching a movie on their central console and just lost control of the car for a moment and happened to swerve to the right. Maybe a fight is going on inside of C4 and a life-or-death struggle for control of the steering wheel is taking place. Maybe I watch too many movies about cars and car chases.

I mentally decided that C4 was swerving to avoid debris and the debris was in the lane ahead toward the left side of the lane. I decided that I would take action before the cascading string of cars ahead of me took their actions. This is a tough call because any of those other cars, the C1, C2, C3, could take evasive action that then gets me into further hot water as I am carrying out my plan of action. I decided that I would instantly switch into the fast lane. I was paying attention and knew that the fast lane was available. I figured that if I got into the fast lane, I would have more room to avoid the debris. I could use the fast lane and the shoulder to the left of the fast lane, if needed, for me to swerve to the left.

Would C1, C2, C3 opt to swerve to the right? If so, my being in the fast lane, on the left of them, would likely make me safer than staying in the slow lane behind them. Any of them could either hit their brakes and I would have possibly slammed into them. Or, any of them could strike the debris and it maybe gets even worse and less avoidable for me, since I am at the end of the pack. By swinging into the fast lane, I hoped that I would avoid the cascading game, I would have more avenues of escape, I would be able to hit my brakes and not have any cars directly ahead of me that I might ram into.

Turns out, all of the above was pretty much correct. It was a remnant of a blown-out tire, sitting in the slow lane, just at the lane markings edge left of the lane. Each of the C1, C2, C3 avoided it by swerving to the right. I avoided it by having gotten into the fast lane and passed it, since it was now to my right. No one got into an accident. I did think though that some other cars going up to this point might fare a different fate. Hoped that the blown-out tire, and the reactions of other human drivers and cars, would not ultimately produce a deadly accident.

I appreciate that you've followed along in my above story about the driving incident. Though it has taken me a little while here to describe the incident, it actually played out in about a handful of seconds of time. Imagine the scenario in your mind. You likely have encountered similar situations. The whole thing happened very quickly. Some say these things are almost like they happened in a dream. Come and gone.

Today's self-driving cars are not doing much about this kind of predictive scenario planning. One would say that most of today's self-driving cars are the "monkey see, monkey do" variety. Whatever is happening directly in front of the self-driving car is the scope of attention of the AI. Does the car immediately ahead swerve or not, does it slow down or speed up, these are the factors used by the AI to decide what action to take for the self-driving car.

Suppose that the driving scenario I just described had happened to a self-driving car. For most self-driving cars today, it would not have particularly noticed that C4 swerved. All the AI would be concentrating on would be that C1 is still driving straight ahead and at the pace of the pack. You might say, well, Lance so what, the AI would have been OK because it would have seen the C1 swerve when it reached the debris and the AI could have commanded the controls of the self-driving car to also swerve. Case closed.

But, I say, suppose the AI did observe C1 swerve, but further it took the AI a few moments to decide to swerve the self-driving car to also avoid the debris. This reaction time might have been so long (a few extra split seconds) that the self-driving car might have hit the debris. We don't know for sure whether hitting the debris would have been disastrous, but we can assume there is some probability that it could have been. Furthermore, the AI for sure would not have had enough time to switch lanes as I had done. This is because I had predicted the future, and it gave me more time to take evasive action.

That's why we are working toward predictive scenario modeling for self-driving cars. Our cars should not be driven by AI that is the equivalent of a child. A child that instantly reacts to something is not what we want our self-driving cars to do. We want our self-driving cars to already know how to predict when that coffee mug that is teetering on the office desk that it will fall to the ground and shatter. Some say that the way that we'll get our AI toward this kind of predictive capability is via deep learning. Deep learning assumes that you have sufficient examples of driving behavior and situations for the AI to find patterns and be able to derive solutions that can then play out in similar scenarios.

That's one way to do it. Another and complimentary way is to have known templates of scenarios, such as my example before about the debris situation. The AI compares the existing situation to an extensive library of templates, trying to see if the scenario is one that has already been identified. This includes using probabilities because the scenarios in-hand are not necessarily going to be identical to the current situation. Likewise, the solutions, such as my swinging into the fast lane, will apply in some circumstances and not in others.

The scenarios are contextually based. The situation of the open highway differs from what happens when driving in the suburbs. It differs from what happens in the city context. Thus, the AI must have scenarios that are contextually aware. The topmost AI strategic planning component of the self-driving car needs to know the existing context to then select among scenarios and apply probabilities based upon the context.

Notice that another facet of the predictive scenario modeling involves looking ahead at the moves and counter moves involved in the actions and counter actions of other drivers. In AI that plays chess, we refer to a look ahead as a ply. The more or deeper you look ahead, the more ply you are examining. At the start of a chess game, you are able after the opening move to consider the next 20 positions possible to respond to the move. After 6 moves, it is something like 9,132,484 positions to explore. The overall aspect is that when the AI of the self-driving car is examining scenarios, it also needs to do a look ahead and the deeper ply it can go, the more it will have to judge what action to take. This though takes more processing time, and as I've indicated during my example, a car scenario plays out in real-time with often just a few seconds available to examine the scenario, make predictions, and then take action to control the car.

I urge other self-driving car makers to also step-up their AI toward doing predictive scenario modeling. Without this, we are not going to get to a true self-driving car, which is referred to as a Level 5. Today's AI "monkey see, monkey do" is barely sufficient to properly and safely operate self-driving cars, since it assumes that if the self-driving car cannot figure out what to do, it merely hands control of the car to the human driver in the car.

By the way, are you wondering what happened in the experiment with the ravens? The experiment tested the ravens to see if they could make tool-use decisions for an event that was 15 minutes in the future (a short-term prediction), and then another round involving an event that was 17 hours in the future (a somewhat longer-term prediction). The ravens seemed to perform pretty well. According to the researchers, the ravens did even better than 4-year-old children that were used as a comparison to the same tasks that the ravens performed.

The jury is still out about making any firm conclusions of raven intelligence and their predictive capabilities (some have criticized various aspects of the raven experiment). Hey, maybe instead of trying to build AI that can drive a self-driving car, we instead train ravens to drive cars. We would then have raven-driven cars. That's a future prediction for you. Well, not very likely, and I hope I've not offended any ravens by saying so (don't want them to come after me when earth becomes the planet of the ravens).

CHAPTER 7

SELFISHNESS
FOR SELF-DRIVING CARS

CHAPTER 7

SELFISHNESS
FOR SELF-DRIVING CARS

You might be aware of this famous movie quote: "Greed, for lack of a better word, is good. Greed is right. Greed works." This was uttered by the fictional character Gordon Gekko in the 1987 movie "Wall Street" and became a rather popular topic of discussion. Some thought it was the perfect way to do things and that we are all and all should be motivated by personal greed, which presumably will in the end be of benefit to not only the individual but to all. Others condemned this way of thinking and argued that it is merely a crass way of trying to excuse "screwing over" the little guy by the big and powerful.

This notion of personal self-interest or personal selfishness is not new. Adam Smith famously became known for the economic theory of the invisible hand. In his 1776 book "The Wealth of Nations," he used the phrase "invisible hand" in one small passage and it has since then become the cornerstone phrase for an entire economic philosophy and spawned much debate.

The concept is that people can go ahead and be selfish and pursue their own particular self-interests, which, though at first glance it might seem like this would not be for the greater good of all, it turns out that it will produce a greater benefit for all (according to those that claim to believe in the invisible hand idea).

What does this have to do with self-driving cars?

A lot. When humans are driving cars, how do they drive their cars? I don't mean how they operate the controls and use the accelerator or brake, but instead I mean what is their behavior as drivers. What motivates them as they drive. Humans are not mindless robots that obey every rule of law while driving. You've certainly witnessed your share of drivers that seem to be rude, they take advantage of situations, they cut-off other drivers, they push into the pack, they hog the road, you name it.

Let me give you an example. Each morning, during my freeway commute, I see drivers that are doing the following. As I near a popular part of Los Angeles, the volume of traffic and the curve of the freeway causes traffic to start to back-up. It is entirely predictable and happens each day, around the same time of day. Driving up to this scene, as a human driver you can see that the traffic ahead of you is starting to get bogged down. It's obvious. Imagine if you were at the grocery store and you could see that lots of people were getting into the cashier lines to pay for their groceries, and you could see that things are starting to pile-up in terms of long lines ahead of you, prior to your getting into line.

Now, the civil way to deal with the upcoming bogged down traffic would be to presumably stay in your respective lane and just gradually enter into the back of the pack. This would be the least disruptive to everyone. Your car and you would be easily predictable. If you are in the fast lane, stay there, and just come to a slowing speed or even stopped in your lane as you near the back of the pack for that particular lane. Likewise, if you are in the slow lane, stay in it, and gently come upon the cars that are up ahead bogged down. This would be similar to the grocery store, wherein you just pick whichever cashier line you happen to be near and get into that line to then ultimately pay for your groceries.

Is this what happens? Do cars stay in their lanes and without much fuss just come upon the back of the pack? Do humans coming up to cashier lines in the grocery store just willingly and without any fuss stand in whatever line they happen to be near? I am betting you would all pretty much agree with me that this is not the way that things go. Instead, it is a madcap free-for-all. It is every man, woman, and child for their own savagery and survival. In the grocery store, I see people dart over to whatever line they think the shortest. But, if they get there and it slows down, they get frustrated and try to sneak over into another line instead.

It is a dog-eat-dog world out there. For the cars, here's what I see happen every morning. A car that's in the fast lane and going at a high speed will dart across several lanes of traffic to get into the slow lane if that lane looks shorter. Cars in the slow lane will try to jam across lanes of traffic and get into the fast lane, if that lane looks shorter. Since no one really knows which lane is the "best" in terms of being able to get through the bogged down traffic, each person is making a personal judgment and deciding which way to go. Thus, you have crazy drivers crisscrossing each other, slow lane drivers nearly colliding with fast lane drivers that are each diving toward the other one's lanes under the assumption that it is better to be in the other lane.

I suppose it looks like frenzied ants. The cars seem to be randomly going this way and that way. Sure, there are a few drivers that opt to stay in their already seated lane, but around them is chaos. A car to your left is trying to squeeze in front of you. A car to your right is trying to go back around you. It is a swirl of cars that are playing a dangerous game.

With this number of cars jockeying across the lanes, you are ultimately going to have someone that slams into someone else. I witness this about once or twice a week, it is a fender bender paradise at this freeway curve. I don't know whether the ones that get their bumpers locked are caught off-guard and this is the first time they had been in this particular bogged down part of the freeway, or whether it is seasoned crazies that finally had statistical chance catch up with them due to their rude behavior repeatedly playing out day after day. If you play with fire, you'll eventually get burned, as they say.

Sadly, it could also be that there are "innocents" that aren't playing the game, and an avid and careless game player rams into them. Thus, those that weren't trying to be selfish get perhaps drawn into it, and get wrecked, by one of those that is. Somehow, I am guessing we'd all wish that it was more like two selfish drivers that smacked into each other. Their just deserves, we'd think.

I am sure that some of you are saying that this is atrocious behavior. Those human drivers should be shot. Well, it depends. If you believe in the Gorden Gekko claim that greed is good, or if you believe that Adam Smith is right about the invisible hand, you would be arguing that the behavior of these drivers is actually a good thing. They are presumably optimizing the roadway use. They are finding a means to get as many cars through the bogged down freeway section as fast as possible. If they instead were "mindless sheep" that stayed in their lanes, you might argue that this would be less effective use of the roadway and be less expeditious overall to the flow of traffic.

Some of you might be pondering this notion. Could it be the case that the selfish driver is actually ensuring that we all benefit? Does the selfishness lead to more effective use of the roadways and shorter drive times for us all? There are many traffic simulations that seem to suggest this is the case. Controversy abounds about this notion, but it is absolutely a consideration and one that many have shown to have merit. We as a society are based on selfish behavior, which manifests itself throughout our lives, and so it makes sense that it would manifest itself in our driving behavior too. We don't become some different person simply because we are seated behind the wheel of a car. We take our biases and our approaches into that driver's seat, and our consequent driving behavior is based on that foundation. Good or bad. Ugly or pretty.

So, should self-driving cars do the same thing? Some AI developers are appalled that I would even ask the question. Their viewpoint is that of course we should not have self-driving cars that behave this way.

In their utopian world, all self-driving cars are civil toward each other. Once we have V2V (vehicle to vehicle) communications, one car will politely say to another car that it wants to change lanes. The other car will politely reply, yes, I am would be happy to help you change lanes. They then offer each other sufficient space to make the lane change. Thank you, says the one car to the other car. It's a wonderful world. I call this the crock world. If this ever does happen, it is many years from now, in some far future that we can't even yet see.

Furthermore, self-driving cars are going to be mixing with other human driven cars for the foreseeable future. The question arises whether the self-driving cars should be the "mindless sheep" and allow the human driven cars to run wild around them. I assert that self-driving cars that are timid will actually make driving conditions worse for us all, and especially human driven cars.

At the Cybernetic Self-Driving Car Institute, we are exploring the infusion of selfishness into self-driving cars. We aim to allow self-driving cars to act in a safe but intentionally selfish manner, which, one could argue will in the end be of benefit to the greater good of society. It's the invisible hand, if you will.

Here's the way it works. When a self-driving car has its selfishness going, it will tend toward making choices that seem to benefit itself the most. Suppose it comes up to a four way stop. Right now, we've had circumstances of a self-driving car that never gets a chance to move forward from a four way stop, due to human drivers being aggressive at the four way stop. The human drivers challenge the self-driving car, doing so by creeping forward at their respective stop sign, which causes the self-driving car to back-down from trying to go forward. In this game of chicken, all the human drivers currently know that the self-driving car will be the chicken and back down.

With a self-driving car that has the selfishness engaged, it will be at the four way stop and be aggressive. It is not going to let other cars intimidate it. It edges forward and makes things clear that it intends to go ahead. If a human driver wants to test the will of the self-driving car, the self-driving car is gladly willing to oblige. Take me on, it is essentially saying to the other drivers. This is what a human driver would do, and so the self-driving car is mimicking that same behavior.

How far does this go? Well, human drivers tend to have thresholds to their selfishness. On my freeway commute, I see most of the self-interested drivers that are crisscrossing lanes, and this is what I would characterize as say average selfishness. You then have a few that go across the selfishness barrier into ultra-selfishness. They go onto the shoulder of the freeway and use it to get ahead of the bogged down traffic. This is blatantly against the law. Each morning, I say a small prayer that a cop will get these drivers. I really wish there was some automatic way to get them targeted and punished for their behavior, maybe even use a laser system to then melts their tires. I can dream, can't I?

Anyway, the point is that when I say that we are using AI to develop selfishness driving behavior, I also want to emphasize that it is something that can be engaged and disengaged, so you can choose when the selfishness arises. Furthermore, it can be scaled to low, medium, or high, meaning that it can be either subtle selfishness, more pronounced selfishness, and can be full selfishness. We aren't though including the ultra-selfishness, though I suppose some would say we should, and we could somewhat easily by allowing the anti-illegal driving routines to let the selfishness override them.

When I mentioned earlier that some AI developers for self-driving cars do not think that self-driving cars should behave selfishly, it is one reason why you aren't yet seeing this kind of behavior emerging in self-driving cars. There are several added reasons. Let's look at them.

Reasons for not allowing selfishness for self-driving cars:

- Because in a utopian world of all self-driving cars they will allow cooperate willingly with each other (far off in the future, maybe never).

- Because some AI developers haven't thought about the selfishness aspects and so they are blissfully unaware of the practical nature of it (hopefully I am getting their attention).

- Because if you believe in Issac Asimov's "Three Rules of Robotics" you would argue that self-driving cars are robots and should abide by Asimov and therefore presumably not be selfish (though, one can argue that Asimov does not tackle this topic per se).

- Because of concern about a public perception backlash (will people tolerate a self-driving car that beats them in a game of chicken).

- Because of the potential for car accidents involving self-driving cars (I've already debunked the idea that it will be zero fatalities once we have self-driving cars, and so the question arises whether there would be a rise in car accidents due to selfish self-driving cars or whether there might be a net reduction).

- Because of not being able to figure out how to include selfishness into self-driving cars (we've got that one covered, it involves using AI techniques accordingly and encompassing behavior modifying routines).

- Because of a fundamental belief that selfishness is bad, no matter what anyone else says about it (this is the camp that doesn't go for the invisible hand).

If you are a self-driving car maker, you can presumably decide whether you want to include selfishness into how your AI and your self-driving car is created. One perspective is that if you don't want it, don't include it. The only rub there is that if you think that maybe consumers will like having such a feature, and if your self-driving car lacks it, then consumers might buy your competitors self-driving car instead.

Thus, another viewpoint for a self-driving car maker would be to include the selfishness capability, so you can say you have it, and be on par with other self-driving car makers, and then allow for it to be used or not used. For usage, it could either be activated by the car owner or occupant, or it could be activated by the AI itself. In essence, you could have the AI determine when selfishness makes sense to use. On my morning commute, the AI might decide for itself that the selfishness will help at the freeway curve, and so invoke the selfishness capability, or it might decide that it isn't worth the added effort and keep the selfishness in a box and awaiting usage for some other occasion or circumstance.

Some might say that we should collectively as a society decide whether to allow self-driving cars to be selfish. Maybe we should have regulations that dictate whether self-driving car makers can include a selfishness component or not. Others think that the self-driving car makers ought to reach their own collective accord on this. Perhaps they all could get together and agree that no one will use selfishness in the AI driving elements of the self-driving car. Or, maybe they agree to allowing it, but then also agree to how it is to be implemented and how far it can go. Maybe this will happen. Probably, the selfishness aspects will arise by happenstance as car makers realize its value. Once enough self-driving cars are on the roads, and if some have selfishness, and if the selfishness leads to accidents or deaths, we'll likely then get a spotlight shined on what this is, how it came to be, and what we'll do about it. Guess we'll wait and see. Or am I being selfish in saying so?

CHAPTER 8
LEAP FROG DRIVING FOR SELF-DRIVING CARS

CHAPTER 8

LEAP FROG DRIVING FOR SELF-DRIVING CARS

Are you familiar with leap frog driving on the highways?

You've probably done this kind of driving and didn't even realize there is a name for it. Here's how it goes. You are driving along on say a highway with two lanes in your direction. The rightmost lane is considered the "slow" lane. The leftmost lane is considered the "fast" lane. Trucks are pretty much supposed to stay in the slow lane. Passenger cars are able to travel in the fast lane.

On the open highway, you see the cars zooming along, using that fast lane to hit 80 miles per hour or more (some daring to go 100 miles per hour). The trucks hauling Wal-Mart goods and Fedex packages are lumbering along in the slow lane, hugging the posted speed limit and daring not to go much faster else they might lose their truckers license. I am sure many look at envy as the cars go past them at what must seem like light speeds in comparison.

A passenger car that is entering into this open highway will usually come into the slow lane. At that point, they need to carefully juggle being in front of a truck that is lumbering along, and then try to find enough of a space to get up-to-speed to merge into the fast lane. Some car drivers are pretty stupid and just bluntly go from the slow lane into the fast lane, and cause other fast lane cars to hit their brakes because the lane switching dolts aren't going the speed of the fast lane. Have you ever honked your horn or given the finger to one of those idiots? Probably. Rightfully, though I am not encouraging road rage.

93

When trying to exit from the open highway, a car going in the fast lane has to maneuver into the slow lane, finding a space between trucks that are lumbering along. The car driver must time this such that they are in the slow lane with enough time to make their upcoming exit. Once again, there are dolts that misjudge this dance. They dart into the slow lane and need to immediately catch the upcoming exit ramp. Meanwhile, they cause the trucks in the slow lane to have to pump on their brakes. I sometimes wish that a truck would just knock one of those cars into the air, and maybe show the driver a lesson. Though I am not encouraging violence of any kind.

So far, we have a two-lane highway in a particular direction, a slow lane to the right, a fast lane to the left, entrance ramps and exit ramps that connect to the slow lane, we have trucks primarily occupying the slow lane, and cars primarily occupying the fast lane. The cars do go into the slow lane, mainly for purposes of entering onto the freeway and then transitioning into the fast lane, or for exiting the highway by first transitioning from the fast lane into the slow lane. Does all of this seem clear cut? I would think you've seen these many times if you've ever driven across a state or similar lengthy driving journey.

Now, let's talk about the leap frog. Suppose you are in the fast lane, and the car ahead of you is not going fast. Or at least not going fast enough to suit you. Sometimes, you'll hug their bumper and hope they get the idea to get out of your way. Sometimes you flash your bright lights of your headlights to clue them to get out of the way. If none of these techniques work, you'll do a leap frog. You look for an opportunity to get into the slow lane. You then proceed ahead of the car that is "blocking" the fast lane, and then get back into the fast lane ahead of the dawdling driver. You just did a leap frog.

We'll use the capital letter F to represent the fast lane, and we'll use the capital letter S to represent the slow lane. You were initially going in the fast lane, lane F, and then you switched into the slow lane, lane S, and then you zipped up ahead and got back into the fast lane, lane F. We could say that you did this sequence: F-S-F. With me on this? You were in the F lane, then S lane, then F lane. This is one type of leap frog. It is the F-S-F leap frog.

Suppose instead you are in the slow lane. You have decided not to use the fast lane per se. You are fine with being in the slow lane with the lumbering trucks. You maybe like this because you don't want to go 100 miles per hour in the fast lane, and know that if you don't do the 100 mph that other idiots in the fast lane that are clearly driving over the speed limit grossly are going to honk their horns or ride your bumper. Those idiots!

But, there you are in the slow lane and stuck behind a truck carrying onions. What a stench! Being behind that truck is just terrible. So, you decide to switch into the fast lane, momentarily. You then drive up ahead of the onion stinking truck. You next switch back into the slow lane, since you don't want to continue occupying the fast lane and become a bottleneck. In this case, you were in the slow lane, lane S, and then switched into the fast lane, lane F, and then after passing the truck you got back into the slow lane, lane S. Let's refer to this as this sequence: S-F-S. With me on this? You were in the S lane, then the F lane, then the S lane. This is another type of leap frog. It is the S-F-S leap frog.

We now have two types of leap frogging, consisting of the F-S-F and the S-F-S.

What's so special about this? Today's self-driving cars can barely do the F-S-F and the S-F-S. Let me explain. The self-driving car of today has AI that pretty much wants to stay in whatever lane it is in. Lane switching is hard. It is dangerous. It takes a lot of additional sensory analysis. We humans take lane switching for granted. The typical self-driving car will only switch lanes if there is a must reason to do so, and often only if prompted by a human to do so. Or, the self-driving car will ask the human driver in the car to get the car into another lane and then the self-driving car will continue from that point. Generally, the self-driving cars of today are not doing a leap frog.

Notice that novice drivers such as teenagers learning to drive are about the same way. They timidly get onto the highway and stay in the slow lane. Making lane changes is frightening. They stay in the slow lane and only venture into the fast lane if prodded to do so. For them, the leap frog is an advanced skill and one they have yet to master. For seasoned drivers, we are used to doing the leap frog. It's considered an essential skill for any sophisticated driver. For seasoned drivers that are perhaps reckless, they do so many leap frogs that they are at times risking themselves and the lives of other drivers.

You might insist that a self-driving car should not do a leap frog, at all. In the utopian world of some self-driving car AI developers, they would say that there isn't a need to do a leap frog. Stay in your lane. Do not switch lanes. Only switch lanes when there is an absolute necessity. If you are in the slow lane, stay there. If you are in the fast lane, stay there. Yes, you can switch from the fast lane to the slow lane, but only because you need to ultimate exit the freeway soon. Yes, you can switch from the slow lane to the fast lane, but only because you have just entered into the freeway.

No self-driving car is supposed to be playing frogger, according to these AI developers. They would also say that once all self-driving cars are on the roads, they will communicate with each other and the world will be a wonderful place. This is because they will in a civil manner always let entering cars to have a gap in the slow lane to get onto the freeway gently and easily. Likewise, they will in a civil manner open a gap for a car in the fast lane that needs to get into the slow lane in order to exit. Well, I am supposing this might someday be true, but not for a long, long time. For many of us, there is going to be a mixture of self-driving cars and human driven cars. And those human driven cars are not going to be so civil.

At the Cybernetic Self-Driving Car Institute, we believe that self-driving cars need to be able to do a leap frog. For some, this is considered an "edge problem." We think that leap frogging is and should be a standard skill in the AI of the self-driving car.

That being said, some right away will argue that we are encouraging bad driving behavior. They complain that we are allowing self-driving cars to do what we don't want human drivers to do. I would say this is an extreme perspective. I think we all would accept that a leap frog is a proper and appropriate maneuver, when done sparingly, when done safely, and when done as the circumstances so arise. If you are saying that the doing lots of leap frogs or doing them without safe driving is bad, I am completely in agreement with you. As I suggested before, there are leap frog idiots that do the leap frog in the worst ways, at the worst times, and endanger us all. Down with the bad leap froggers.

What happens when a self-driving car wants to do a leap frog? It's pretty complicated, but can be done using the other fundamentals that a self-driving car should already be equipped with. For the S-F-S, the self-driving car is in the slow lane, and it wants to get into the fast lane. This requires detecting the cars that are in the fast lane. Is there an available gap to get into the fast lane? Is there a car coming up in the fast lane that the self-driving car will inadvertently cut-off, if so, wait for the next opportunity. Can the self-driving car get enough speed to get out of the slow lane and into the fast lane, doing so without becoming a bottleneck in the fast lane?

At this point, assume that the self-driving car has done the first part, the S and F of the S-F-S sequence. How far is the self-driving car next going to need to go in the fast lane, since remember that its goal at this point is to get back into the slow lane at the earliest opportunity. So, now that the self-driving car has made its way into the fast lane, it is inching ahead of whatever was in the way in the slow lane, and then looking to get back into the slow lane. This might mean getting in front of the truck that was in the slow lane. Or, it might require going further up ahead, maybe getting ahead of several trucks, and then finding an opening to get back into the slow lane. Notice all of the judgment required in this. It is not a mathematical formula that applies across all situations. Instead, the self-driving car AI has to be taking a step-by-step, predictive and planned approach.

The distances matter in the leap frog. Sometimes, it is a quick leap frog. Tracing the S-F-S, you quickly get into the fast lane from the slow lane, you zip ahead of a truck, you then quickly jump back into the slow lane. We'll refer to the distances by using the number 1 to mean a short distance, and we'll use the letter N to denote a longer distance. We'll add to our denotations by saying that a S1-F1-S1 means a maneuver of a leap frog in which we did a quick step for each of the S, F, and S. The opposite extreme would be the SN-FN-SN, which would mean that you went a long distance to maneuver into the fast lane from the slow lane, and then a long distance to maneuver out of the fast lane and back into the slow lane, and that you then continued in the slow lane for a long distance.

What's the purpose for these? We can now describe the various leap frogs.

They are:

S1-F1-S1
S1-FN-S1
S1-F1-SN
SN-F1-S1
SN-FN-S1
SN-FN-SN

The AI system needs to know how to do each of these maneuvers to properly execute the S-F-S leap frog.

Likewise, there is this:

F1-S1-F1
F1-SN-F1
F1-S1-FN
FN-S1-F1
FN-SN-F1
FN-SN-FN

The AI system needs to know how to do each of those maneuvers to properly execute the F-S-F leap frog.

When I was driving from Los Angeles to Silicon Valley recently, which is about a six-hour drive, I counted how many leap frogs I did. In this case, I was not in a hurry to get to my destination, so I opted to not do many leap frogs. I counted about 20 over the entire driving journey. That's about 3 leap frogs per hour.

On the way back, I was in a hurry to get back to Los Angeles. I knew that the leap frogs could speed up my driving journey. I did nearly 60 leap frogs. That's about 10 per hour, or one every six minutes of driving time.

In the first journey, heading up to Silicon Valley, there was a lot of time separation between each leap frog. On the return journey, I was actually doing leap frogs one immediately after another.

Let's consider this sequence.

F1: S1: F1 / F1:S1:FN / F1:SN:FN / FN:S1:F1 / FN:S1:FN

Notice that I was trying to stay out of the slow lane for any length of time. I wanted to get into the slow lane just so I could pass a car in the fast lane that was blocking the fast lane and that idiot driver didn't want to get out of the way. I would jump into the slow lane, and out of the slow lane, as quickly as possible (they all were S1's, except for one that was an SN). The reason I had an SN in that sequence was that I got into the slow lane to make my passing maneuver, but then other cars in the fast lane were coming up so quickly that I could not safely get back into the fast lane. Thus, I paid the penalty of being stuck in the slow lane.

This is an important point. Some human drivers think that if they do the leap frogs that they will always do better than not doing the leap frogs. This is not necessarily the case. You probably see drivers all the time that seem to jump into another lane, and they think they will do the leap frog, but they get stuck in the other lane. You meanwhile pass them, laughing at their stupidity for poorly using the leap frog technique.

Another thing I'll bet you do is play mind games with other drivers that are doing leap frogs. For example, you can see a driver in the fast lane that is itching to get around a car ahead of them in the fast lane. Suppose you are in the slow lane and nearly paralleling the driver desiring to do a leap frog. They are trying to eye whether to get into the slow lane just ahead of you, or just behind you. They really don't want to get behind you because you might be a bottleneck. On the other hand, if you are moving fast enough to go past the dolt blocking

---

the fast lane, then the leap frog ready driver figures it is worth getting behind you.

You can then egg on the leap frog desiring driver by purposely making it seem that you are proceeding fast enough to pass the dolt in the fast lane. The leap frogger then makes their move behind you. At this point, you gradually slow down, just enough that it is apparent that you are not going to be passing the dolt in the fast lane. Now the leap frogger gets frustrated because they committed to get behind you, but it's not working out well.

They then give up the leap frog per se and get back into the fast lane, hoping they can ride the bumper of the dolt to get them out of the way. You could leave things alone, but you want to continue the mind game. You therefore tease the leap frogger by leaving just a minimal amount of space ahead of you that the leap frogger thinks they can maybe make the play that way. But, it's not enough space. You then move up ahead and parallel the dolt, and even start to edge ahead of him. This is likely enough to entice the leap frog into trying again by getting behind you.

If you are clever enough, you can torture the leap frogger for miles and miles on this. When I say clever enough, I mean do this without getting caught and never letting the leap frogger get ahead. But, be forewarned that if the leap frogger thinks you are intentionally impeding them, it can become deadly serious. They will try to swing at your car or otherwise possibly threaten you. You have to do this without appearing to do it. The leap frogger thinks it is just random driving and not driving with mind games.

Well, I should emphasize that the above is not recommended at all. This is playing perilous games at high speeds with multi-ton objects that can kill those around them. Do not do any of the above. I say that, but I assure you there are drivers constantly doing it.

I certainly don't want self-driving cars to play those games.

But, I tell you about this because I want to emphasize something else about the leap frog. So far, I have indicated that it is a technique that any good self-driving car should know how to do. That's true. There is the other side of this coin, namely that other cars are going to do leap frogs. Thus, the self-driving car should be aware of other cars that are trying to do a leap frog.

You might wonder, why does it matter if the AI knows that another car is doing a leap frog? Why not just let the other car, whether human driven or self-driving, do its leap frog. This is somewhat the case, but not entirely. If you as a human driver see someone doing a leap frog, you can either inhibit them by getting in their way (as I've described above), or you could just drive along without noticing and let them do whatever they are going to do, or you could actually help them.

I usually try to help someone doing a leap frog. I do this not so much for their benefit, but for mine. I don't want a leap frog that gets impatient to maybe make a mistake during the leap frog. I would rather they have plenty of clearance and can do the leap frog, even if they are inept at it.

For example, the other day, while driving at 80 miles per hour, a driver decided to do a leap frog, directly in front of me. Unfortunately, the idiot was not thinking clearly. I was in the slow lane, he was in the fast lane. He timed it poorly and tried to get into the slow lane just as I was nearing a truck up ahead. He wanted to get into my slow lane, move ahead, swing back into the fast lane, but do it before he ran into the back of the truck. I could see that we was not going to make it. So, I slowed down while in the slow lane and gave him a larger space to make his play. I didn't have to do it, but I knew that he was going to otherwise turn things dangerous.

We therefore should expect this:

- Self-driving car should be able to do a leap frog
- Self-driving car should be able to do the S-F-S leap frog
- Self-driving car should be able to do the F-S-F leap frog
- Self-driving car should be able to recognize a leap frog being done by another car
- Self-driving car should be able to aid a leap frog being done by another car
- Self-driving car should be able to do all variants of the S-F-S
- Self-driving car should be able to do all variants of the F-S-F
- Self-driving car should be able to do strings of S-F-S maneuvers
- Self-driving car should be able to do strings of F-S-F maneuvers

In essence, a savvy self-driving car AI should know about leap frogs, and be able to be proactive and use a leap frog when relevant, and be able to respond or be reactive to someone else doing a leap frog. Next time you are driving on the open highway, be thinking about the leap frog. You might have figured out the leap frog by your own trial-and-error. Now you know that it's a thing. It's a thing that humans do, and that self-driving cars need to be aware of and be able to do too. This applies to mainly the true self-driving car, a Level 5, but can apply to the other levels of self-driving cars too.

CHAPTER 9

PROPRIOCEPTIVE INERTIAL MEASUREMENT UNITS (IMU) FOR SELF-DRIVING CARS

CHAPTER 9

PROPRIOCEPTIVE INERTIAL MEASUREMENT UNITS (IMU) FOR SELF-DRIVING CARS

Where are you, right now?

Are you standing up, sitting down, or laying down? Where were you thirty seconds ago? Where were you thirty minutes ago? Presumably, you are able to answer these questions. You should be able to. Your mind and body are keeping track of your position and movements, doing so without you necessarily being fully aware that it is taking place. Sometimes, such as if you stand-up and try to balance on one leg, you suddenly are aware of your body status, leaning slightly one way and then back the other way. This ability to keep track of your body and where you are is a standard feature of our bodies and involves a close coupling between aspects of your anatomy and your brain.

There's actually a special word for this, it's called your proprioception, and you have proprioceptors that do this work for you. Most people don't realize it's a thing. It is a thing. It's an important thing. You need this to keep track of your physical navigation in the world.

And, it's something that self-driving cars need to have too.

At the Cybernetic Self-Driving Car Institute, we've been developing and expanding the ability of self-driving cars to include proprioception. For humans, we use bodily information that comes from your muscles, your tendons, and other internal organs to keep track of your movement and position (along with your brain, of course). For self-driving cars, the device that provides that same kind of tracking of movement and position is called an Inertial Measurement Unit (IMU). Any bona fide self-driving car has one.

There are various sensory devices on self-driving cars (see my article on sensor fusion for self-driving cars). The most obvious sensors are those such as radar to detect objects, LIDAR to likewise detect objects, sonar for tracking objects, etc. Since we're now using a big word in proprioception, let's add to our vocabulary and we'll refer to those sensors such as radar, LIDAR, sonar as exteroceptors. For humans, exteroceptors are your nose, ears, eyes, and the like, which have to do with sensing information that originates outside of your human body. That's what radar, LIDAR, and sonar do for a self-driving car, they sense information outside of the car.

The IMU is a proprioceptor that keeps track of where the self-driving car is, and does so by movement of the self-driving car (it is considered "inside" info versus the exteroceptors that are collecting "outside" info). You might say to me, Lance, we already have something to readily keep track of a car, namely a GPS system. Yes, a Global Positioning System (GPS) is indeed another device used by a self-driving car. It is another essential device, for sure. Using access to the Global Navigation Satellite System (GNSS), you can keep track generally of where your car is. We use this in everyday cars. We use this in our cell phones and have it so we can pull up a map and see where we are. It is used extensively by ride sharing services such as Uber, showing you where you are and where your ride is.

Have you ever though had your GPS either not work or work in a spotty way? You must have. I am sure you've experienced circumstances wherein your said something like "I am getting a lousy signal" and your GPS was wrong or inaccurate. I was in downtown San Francisco the other day on a quick work trip there, and when I tried to use Uber (this is not an advertisement for them, use whichever ride sharing service you like!), it turned out that the driver thought I was a block away from where I was actually standing. We normally expect our GPS to be within a few feet or meters of accuracy. In this case, it was nearly a city block off.

This makes sense that the GPS would be a kilter. I was standing in a dense downtown area and surrounding me were very tall skyscrapers. The signals for GPS come from orbiting satellites and so any dense object can block or distort the signals. Skyscrapers are certainly highly dense objects, usually composed of masses of metal and steel. Another place that you probably have experienced difficulties using your GPS would be inside a tunnel. If you go into a subway system, bringing up your GPS will usually show a very generalized indication of your location and not be especially accurate.

Believe it or not, your GPS can be distorted by other aspects such as trees. What, you ask, trees? Yes, if you are in a dense wooded area, the trees can also impact the reception of the signals from the satellites. Even clouds and rain can also impact your GPS. Not only can all of these conditions block the signals, it can allow them to pass but cause them to be delayed. You might not have noticed this. If you watch your GPS for a few minutes continuously, you will sometimes notice that it is tracking you step by step, but then seems to jump a step. This is due to a delay as a result of some object that momentarily blocked the signal.

The point to this lengthy lesson about GPS is that simply stated the GPS in your car is not entirely reliable for purposes of knowing where the car is. The GPS signals can be blocked entirely or delayed in their arrival. If you are walking on the street, you might be satisfied with a momentary blockage or delay that's a second or two, or maybe a fraction of a second. If you're in a car, and the car is traveling at 80 miles per hour, do you know how many feet your car travels in one second? Take a guess. Ready for the answer? Your car travels about 117 feet.

Traveling 117 feet per second, and not knowing where your car is because the GPS is blocked or delayed, it's not much of a problem when you as a human are driving a car. You are still aware of what is going on around the car. But, for a self-driving car, not knowing where the car is for 117 feet because there has been a GPS delay is a really bad thing. The virtual model that the AI is keeping of where the self-driving car is, and where other objects are, and where those objects are headed, and where the self-driving car is headed, all of those can get out of sync.

This could be so bad that your self-driving car could get itself into an accident. In essence, it will have lost its way in space and time, for a substantive distance and time, and the ability of the sensors and the AI to deal with that lost perception of body and movement is something we want to try and prevent from happening.

That's why we need an IMU.

An Inertial Measurement Unit (IMU) is a device that is mounted in a fixed position within the body of your self-driving car. It needs to be in a fixed position of the car, so that it is aware of where its anchored placement is. From this fixed position within the car, the IMU will keep track of the movement and position of the car. Usually consisting of several gyroscopes and accelerometers, the IMU provides to the AI of the car an indication of the pitch, role, and heading of the self-driving car (these are referred to as rotational parameters as sourced by the gyroscopes), and also tracks the linear acceleration of the vehicle (that's by the accelerometers).

The reason there are several gyroscopes and several accelerometers in the IMU is to ensure redundancy. Let's suppose we have an IMU that contains three gyroscopes and three accelerometers. We can ask each gyroscope what it is sensing, and compare them to ensure they are all consistent. If one of them differs, we could infer that it has somehow gotten out of tune or maybe is broken. We could then rely on just the other two gyroscopes. Same story for the accelerometers. We have each accelerometer telling what it knows, and if there seems to be a problem with one of them then we have the other two as a failsafe form of redundancy.

You might be thinking that if the self-driving car has an IMU then maybe it does not need the GPS. Why have both, you ask? Having both is crucial. They work hand-in-hand. The IMU can only tell you relative position and movement. The GPS tells you so-called absolute position and movement. What's the difference? The GPS is saying where you specifically are. The IMU tells you how far you've moved from some other position.

For example, the GPS tells me that I am physically standing in Disneyland at coordinates of a certain latitude and longitude. With my eyes, I can see that I am standing near the statue of Walt Disney that resides in front of the Sleeping Beauty Castle. For the IMU, if I had been originally standing at the Walt Disney statue, and I had then walked away from it, the IMU would be able to have indicated that I had walked at a certain angle from that starting position and that I had gone a certain distance which can be calculated based on parameters associated with me and the IMU.

The IMU cannot tell the self-driving car where the self-driving car is per se. Instead, the IMU can tell the self-driving car what has happened in terms of movement and position on a relative basis from some starting point. The IMU is providing the angular velocity and linear acceleration, which can be used to calculate where I am, relative to where I was. For those of you that have ever gone camping with the Boy Scouts or Girl Scouts, you might know this as dead reckoning. Or, if you are sailor, you certainly know about dead reckoning. Dead reckoning is the act of identifying a known starting location and then keeping track of where you have gone over time as relative to that starting position.

In the woods, you might tell the scouts to set as a starting point a large boulder. Then, you ask them to walk a distance away from the boulder, but as they do so, keep track of the angle that they have walked and how many paces they walked. Based on their paces, you would have previously measured their gait, suppose they go a distance of 3 feet for each step, you could then calculate where you are now, relative to where the boulder is.

You need to have some good starting position for the use of dead reckoning. For the IMU in your self-driving car, it will use the GPS to provide that starting position. Let's suppose the GPS says that your self-driving car is at a stated latitude and longitude. The IMU uses that as a stated starting position. The self-driving car then drives for a few seconds. The IMU is keeping track of the rotational parameters and the acceleration. The AI of the self-driving car is getting this fed to it by the IMU. Based on the data from the IMU, the AI can update the virtual model of where the self-driving car is.

The IMU is providing this relative position data continuously. Anyone that has ever done dead reckoning knows that one of the pitfalls of dead reckoning is that there can be errors that accumulate over time and so your relative position can become murky. For the scouts, I mentioned that we'd keep track of their number of steps and then use that to calculate the distance walked. Each step is not exactly the same amount of distance. Thus, when we multiply out the number of steps times what we assume the average step length to be, we are introducing an error since this is only an estimate of the actual distance gone.

The IMU and the AI might be using the circumference of the wheels of the car, along with the number of wheel rotations, in order to estimate the distance traveled. This is equivalent to using the number of steps of the scouts and an estimate of how far they travel with each step. The IMU uses some kind of predetermined algorithm to help translate its gyroscope and accelerometer readings into something that can be used by the AI to ascertain the position of the self-driving car.

I had stated that the GPS and the IMU work hand-in-hand. Let's see why this is indeed the case. The GPS says the self-driving car is at a stated latitude and longitude. Assume the GPS signal is strong and so the AI believes that the latitude and longitude is correctly indicated. The self-driving car moves ahead as directed by the AI. During the next say two seconds, we don't have a GPS signal because it is blocked by tall buildings. Meanwhile, the IMU has been continuously reporting in real-time. The AI is updating the virtual model and believes that the self-driving car is now at position X and Y, relative to the latitude and longitude that it had earmarked two seconds ago.

As you can see, the self-driving car knows where it is, even though the GPS has been blocked for two seconds. While the GPS was being blocked, the IMU was indicating where the self-driving car has moved on a relative position from the "starting point" of the last reliably reported latitude and longitude. Let's pretend that after those two seconds has elapsed, the GPS now reports the latest latitude and longitude and that the signal is strong and reliable. The AI can then update itself and see how far afield it is from where it thought it was. We now have also a new "starting position" since the latest GPS coordinates can be used instead of the coordinates from two seconds ago.

Therefore, the GPS is augmented by what the IMU has to say, and when the GPS is not available the IMU is still allowing us to keep track of where the self-driving car is. In fact, the IMU can be used to always try to verify that the GPS is being accurate, since you could be double-checking the GPS against whatever the IMU has been saying. If we decide that a starting position is when we begin our driving journey, we could be collecting the IMU data throughout the trip and be using it to always try and double-check what the GPS is stating. Of course, we need to keep in mind the "errors" that accumulate when using dead reckoning, and over any substantive length of time and distance those will be relatively large.

Another purpose of the IMU is to allow the AI to determine the slip angle of the self-driving car. The slip angle is an indication of whether the car is maybe skidding, maybe spinning, or maybe tending toward rolling over. The IMU provides the rolling wheel actual direction versus where the wheel is pointing. You've likely experienced this aspect when driving on a slick road.

You might have the wheels pointed toward the left, but the car is actually moving or skidding toward the right. You've lost control of the steering since the tires don't have sufficient traction on the road surface. Remember how they say that you should then turn the wheels in the direction of actual travel and try to regain control of the steering? That's something that the AI needs to be aware of since it too is trying to drive the car as a human would.

The IMU provides to the AI a sense of whether the self-driving car is getting itself into a posture that needs special attention. Imagine you are driving a car and you come off the freeway at a high rate of speed. The off-ramp is curved. You've likely had that scary sensation that the car felt like it was going to tip over as you took that curve, because you were going faster than recommended and the physics of the car and the curve and the road and your speed are tending to tip over the car. As a human, you could feel that sensation of tipping.

The AI needs to be able to have that same sensation. It needs to know whether the car is maybe tipping over. If so, the AI would try to control the car to prevent the car from rolling over. The IMU provides the sensory information for the AI to figure this out. The IMU is pretty handy, since it can be used to keep track of location as done in conjunction with the GPS, and it can also be used to detect circumstances involving the car skidding, spinning, or tipping over. The IMU can be rather precise in its measurements, including within a centimeter of precision, such as tracking the velocity to a 2 centimeter per second accuracy level (or better).

Some like to refer to the IMU as the inner ear of a self-driving car. When the AI is doing sensor fusion, the GPS and the IMU are considered crucial to knowing where the car is, where the car has been, and where the car is headed. We all know about a GPS because we see it on our phones and on displays in our cars. Few know about the IMU. It is one of those silent "organs" deep within the car and that the AI needs to know about on behalf of the humans in the self-driving car and being able to drive the car for them.

For humans, we have our own IMU in that our muscles and tendons, working with our brain, telling us the same kind of relative position and movement information. Any AI developer that is doing systems for self-driving cars should be aware of the important dance between the GPS and the IMU. If you've never heard of the IMU, you might fall off your chair to know that it exists. Of course, your proprioceptors will let you know as you begin to tip off the chair and head to the floor. It won't cushion the blow, but at least your mind can get ready for the floor, command your arms to catch you, and you'll be less likely to get hurt. The hero here was the IMU!

CHAPTER 10

ROBOJACKING

OF

SELF-DRIVING CARS

Lance B. Eliot

CHAPTER 10

ROBOJACKING OF SELF-DRIVING CARS

Carjacking was a new term added to our vocabulary back in the early 1990s. The original case that led to the terminology involved the murder of a female drugstore cashier in Detroit that had refused to give over her car to a hijacker and he shot her dead for her refusal. A newspaper picked up the story and called it a carjacking.

For the next several years, we seemed to have somehow gotten into a national frenzy in the United States of having carjackings. Some estimates indicate that we had about 40,000 carjackings a year, lasting throughout the 1990s. It was so prominent and prevalent that Congress even proposed and passed the Federal Anti-Car Theft Act of 1992, known as FACTA. It became a federal crime to carjack and allowed for a punishment of fifteen years to life for using a firearm to steal a car from someone.

During the height of the evil fad, I remember vividly something that happened to an executive at a major firm in downtown Los Angeles that I knew well and for which I was doing consulting work for his firm. We had been both working together late one night, and I finally told him that I'd have to head home to see my kids before they finished up the night and they went to bed (I always strived to get home and tuck the kids in, and usually tell a bedtime story, about self-driving cars, naturally). He said he'd be leaving shortly after I left. The company was a well-known company and located in a good part of downtown.

I saw him the next day at work, and he had an incredible story to tell. When he had finally left work, he drove off the gate guarded parking lot and drove directly to the freeway. Once on the freeway, he realized that his car was very low on gasoline. He figured that if he saw a gas station right next to the freeway, it would be safe to exit the freeway, drive immediately to the gas station, get some gas, and then get back onto the freeway and be on his way. The whole act should take maybe three to four minutes maximum. He saw a lit-up gas station billboard and it looked like the gas station was seemingly safe, and so he exited the freeway to get his gas.

He pulled up to the gas pumps. There was no one else getting gas. It was late at night. It was not the best part of Los Angeles, but he figured he was right near the freeway and things seemed very quiet at the gas station. As he started to pump gas into his car, which was an expensive foreign model car, another car pulled into the gas station. It pulled up next to where he was standing. Out jumps a guy with a gun. The gunman pointed the gun at him and demanded his wallet. He handed over his wallet, figuring it wasn't worth the chance of dying just to keep his wallet.

The gunman then asked for the keys to the car. He handed over the keys. The gunman got into the car and drove off. My colleague and friend stood there in the gas station, shocked. In less than one minute, he had his life threatened, he'd given up his wallet with all of his private info in it, and he had his car stolen. So much for the idea that by doing a quick gas station stop in just three to four minutes that nothing bad could happen. He was lucky to be alive.

In case you are curious about what happened next, here's the next twist to the story. He called his wife right away to tell her what had happened. Just after doing so, the police called his wife. Turns out that the gunman had driven a few blocks away and ran through a stop sign. A police car was there and the police stopped the vehicle. They got the gunman out of the car, found the wallet, realized that the car wasn't owned by the guy driving it, and so they used the car registration info to give a call to my colleague's home. His wife answered the phone. Imagine if he had not already called her. She would have gotten a call from the police, they would have told her they have a man with a gun that has her husband's wallet and his car. She would have likely assumed he was dead in a ditch somewhere.

Anyway, carjackings still happen and they occur throughout the world. Some countries are faced with lots of carjackings. Some of the carjackings are random in nature, wherein the evil doer just seizes upon a particular random opportunity and takes a car from someone by force. In other cases, it is a planned activity. For example, it is something that mobsters or kidnappers will plan carefully as to when the mark will be in their car and how to best take them and their car.

What does this have to do with self-driving cars?

Answer, there are predictions that self-driving cars will also be attacked by carjackers. In fact, the world has gained a new term for this, it is called robojacking.

The term has not yet made the big time of formally being adopted by the top standard dictionaries, and you'd more likely find it in an urban dictionary. Most are using the word robojacking to refer to hijacking a self-driving car, but others say it is more broadly a term for hijacking anything that is a smart autonomous device, even including an autonomous vacuum cleaner. For purposes herein, let's use robojacking for denoting hijacking of a self-driving car.

The "robo" part of robojacking is intended to suggest that the self-driving car is being driven by a robot. We know that this is not the way that self-driving cars are going, in the sense that there won't be an actual robot that sits in the driver's seat of the car. Instead, the AI of the self-driving car is embedded within the car and its many computer processors. We'll be lenient and use the word "robo" to imply that the self-driving car is not being human driven and instead being driven by a robotic like system, the AI of the self-driving car.

Is robojacking the same as carjacking? In many ways, it is. The same situations that involve getting carjacked can happen likewise for robojacking. We'll take a look at the standard ways in which police advise you to avoid getting carjacked, and see if they apply to robojacking.

- **Try not to drive in bad areas where crime is rampant**

This equally is good advice for anyone in a self-driving car as it would be for a human driven car.

I suppose the main difference will be that when a human is driving a car, and even if they are using a GPS, they are usually nonetheless paying attention to the surrounding area of where they are driving.

When in a self-driving car, you might become so focused on doing things inside the self-driving car as an occupant, and since there is no human driver, you might not be aware of where the car is going per se during the journey to your destination.

This can be somewhat readily resolved by having the self-driving car route around or away from bad areas. Also, the self-driving car could be using its own capabilities to detect the surroundings and if it begins to detect graffiti and other signals or signs that the area is bad, it could automatically reroute.

At the Cybernetics Self-Driving Car Institute, we are exploring these kinds of augmented capabilities for the AI of the car, in order to make it more aware of the driving journey and minimize the chances of a robojacking. As you'll see next, there are many added ways to do this.

- **When stopped in traffic, keep some distance between your vehicle and the vehicle ahead of you.**

This advice is based on the notion that if someone tries to come up to your car and point a gun at you, you could maneuver the car out of traffic and try to drive away. Of course, if the gunman wants to shoot you, this could lead to getting shot right away. It's a trade-off, but anyway, it seems like generally good advice that you would want to have avenues of escape.

This is readily adapted for self-driving cars. If an occupant is worried about being robojacked, the self-driving car could be on alert such that the AI makes sure to be calculating ways to keep from having the self-driving car get pinned. Furthermore, the AI could be continuously identifying ways to escape and get the self-driving car out of a bad situation.

How would the self-driving car know that it is time to escape? This can involve the occupant talking with the self-driving car.

- **Park your car in well-lighted areas that seem safe**

For human drivers, it's certainly good advice to always try to park in a well-lit area and do so in as safe a spot as you can find. I knew one driver that always would park his car under a street light, hoping that the light would discourage anyone from either harming his car or stealing it. I am not sure that it made a difference, but one thing that did happen was kind of ironic. One day, he came out to his beloved car, and someone had tossed a rock at the street light, shattering all the glass and it came down directly onto the hood of his car. As I say, somewhat ironic that his method of trying to be safe had led to this.

For self-driving cars, I've already discussed about improvements as to how self-driving cars will get better and better at parking a car. One aspect that most of the self-driving car makers are not considering involves the choice of where to park a car. In other words, they leave it to the human occupant to tell the self-driving car where to park, and then the self-driving car dutifully parks in that spot.

I've already been saying that we've got to make self-driving cars smarter in that they should also be able to identify where to park. No need to burden the occupant. That being said, this does not preclude allowing the occupant to indicate where they want to park. It is just as though you had a chauffeur that was driving your car for you. You might normally allow the chauffeur to figure out where to park the car, but other times you might indicate to the chauffeur a specific spot that you desire.

A self-driving car could use the clues of the surrounding to try and gauge how safe the parking location is. The lighting can be detected by the camera of the self-driving car. Are there other equally the same cars as your car that are parked there? The image analysis capabilities of the AI can try to ascertain that aspect. We often look to see if other cars similar to our car are parked someplace, figuring that it must be likely "safe" if other cars of the same kind are parked there. And so on.

- **Keep the car windows up and the doors locked**

This piece of conventional advice is a somewhat broad generalization. Yes, I think we all now agree that you should keep your car doors locked at all times. We've gotten used to this as a common feature of any modern car. The part about keeping the windows up is though the over-the-top part. Are we to never allow our windows to be down?

One approach would be that if the car is in motion over a certain speed, say over 5 miles per hour, maybe then the windows can be down. Once the car gets into lower speeds, maybe have the windows automatically roll-up.

This could also be varied by the surroundings. If you are driving in Beverly Hills, maybe the windows can be down. If you are driving in a rougher part of town, perhaps the AI will automatically roll-up the windows. This is something that the AI would likely want to mention to the occupants, so they don't get into a war with the AI about rolling down and rolling up the windows.

- **If you are confronted and have no viable recourse, get out and give up the car**

This piece of advice is one that makes pretty good sense. Is it worth it to die for keeping possession of your car? Probably not. If there is no other evasive maneuver to prevent the carjacking or robojacking, maybe just give up the car and get away as quickly as you can.

For a human driven car, it means that the carjacker can just jump into the driver's seat, and assuming the keys are in the car, they can drive away the car.

For self-driving cars, we're going to have some interesting twists. First, as I've mentioned in the chapter on in-car commands, we don't yet know how one will direct a self-driving car to drive. If a self-driving car is only responsive to say your face due to facial recognition or your voice due to voice recognition, the self-driving car is not going to go anywhere, unless the robojacker keeps you in the self-driving car.

This is bad, of course, because it suggests that robojackers will be more determined to keep the occupant rather than let them go. In essence, if the robojacker cannot drive away your car, as they can now, they will have more incentive to keep you as a hijacked victim.

For self-driving cars, we could have a capability wherein the occupant that does have the right to tell the self-driving car what to do might also have the ability to transfer that designation or to make it an open designation. Thus, it might be that the occupant could tell the self-driving car to take commands from anyone else, and therefore the robojacker does not need necessarily to keep the occupant kidnapped.

Let's suppose that we add such a feature to self-driving cars. There are some other twists involved. By-and-large, self-driving cars are going to be connected with some main servers that are used by a car maker to communicate with the self-driving car. This is done to share the experiences of other self-driving cars with your self-driving car, improving the capability of your self-driving car in a collective manner.

Anyway, presumably, if you got out of your self-driving car, and handed it over to a robojacker, and they drove off, you could simply and easily contact the car maker (or whomever is connected with your self-driving car), and they could then track where the self-driving car goes. They could then alert the police to go pick-up that evil doer. Some even speculate that we might have the self-driving car be told by the server to drive directly to the nearest police station. This would hand-over the evil doer to the police without any kind of police chase.

Is the public ready for this Big Brother kind of capability? Will car makers resist allowing the government to be able to access info about the self-driving cars they have on the roads? Will they allow the government to be able to control those self-driving cars remotely? We are all still today just trying to figure out whether we want the government to look at our Facebook pages or be able to crack into our encrypted iPhones. This whole aspect about self-driving cars and privacy is going to be another substantial can of worms. Mark my words!

Now, so far, I've covered the usual kinds of advice about avoiding carjacking, and compared it to robojacking. There are some that express concern of another kind related to robojacking.

Here's one for will maybe become a favorite evil doer practice:

- **Stand in front of a self-driving car to make it come to a halt, then robojack it**

Currently, most of the self-driving cars are very timid when it comes to taking action after detecting a pedestrian in front of the car. The self-driving car will come to a halt and do whatever it can to avoid hitting the pedestrian. There is an ongoing ethics debate about how self-driving cars should be programmed in terms of the potential for harming humans.

Suppose you are robojacker. Suppose you know that self-driving cars won't harm a pedestrian. You therefore walk straight up to a self-driving car and stand in front of it. You know it won't try to run you over. If it was a human driver, you wouldn't be so sure. You would realize that a human driver might just floor the gas and try to run you over. It becomes a game of chicken to see who blinks first. Does the gunman try to shoot the human driver, or does the human driver hope they can run over the gunman before they can get off a shot.

With the self-driving car, there is presumably no longer a game of chicken. The robojacker knows that the self-driving car won't try to run them over. They could have an accomplice that stands in front of the self-driving car, which comes to screeching halt because the AI has been programmed to do so, and let's say the gunman is maybe standing just aside of the self-driving car, gun ready and aimed at the occupants. This seems like a pretty easy way to robojack.

The question then arises as to whether we want our self-driving cars to be so timid. Suppose we allow our self-driving cars to be more aggressive. If it believes that a robojacking is taking place, maybe it indeed proceeds as though it is intending to run over the pedestrian. How does it know though that this is robojacking and maybe not just someone kidding around? Can the AI be good enough to differentiate those situations that are dire from those that are not? We could have the human occupant offer a verbal command to the self-driving car, whereby they tell the self-driving car whether it is a robojacking or not. If they say it is, then perhaps the self-driving car gets aggressive. But suppose now the occupant is kidding and didn't really mean to say that it is a robojacking. I think you can see the conundrum here.

Of course, even human drivers are apt to do the same thing that the AI would do. We don't know that all humans would try to run over a gunman. Some might, some might not.

Similarly, another style of robojacking might be when a car in front of the self-driving car comes to a halt to pin in the self-driving car, with another accomplice in car behind the self-driving car. This can happen with human driven cars and so there is not really much difference, other than again the effort to try and escape, which as mentioned we could have the AI try to do.

Some are worried that with self-driving cars that the occupants are going to be sitting ducks, as though being in a self-driving car makes them be this way. I don't think this seems to make much sense. They are no more sitting ducks than would be with a human driven car. We can program the AI to be as much loose and "dangerous" of a driver as a human driver, if we want to do so. Indeed, we've been programming our AI to be able to play chicken with someone standing in front of a car. It is readily doable.

Right now, self-driving car makers are being extremely cautious and making the self-driving cars as timid as possible. I've already mentioned that pedestrians can play games with self-driving cars by approaching a self-driving car to get it to stop.

This is really the nature of today's primitive approaches, and I seriously doubt we're going to keep that same approach as self-driving cars get smarter and more prevalent.

Is robojacking something to be afraid of? Are we going to see a rampant new era of robojackings that will rival the 1990s era of carjackings? I don't think we will.

That being said, I'd like to add that if we do nothing to prepare self-driving cars for robojackings, yes, we'd be setting ourselves up for this unfortunate wave of crime. On the other hand, I'd hope that as AI developers and self-driving car makers we will be wise enough to anticipate robojackings and try to reduce the chances of it becoming a thing. Let's all strive for that.

CHAPTER 11

SELF-DRIVING CAR IS A MOONSHOT AND MOTHER OF ALL AI PROJECTS

CHAPTER 11

SELF-DRIVING CAR IS A MOONSHOT
AND MOTHER OF ALL AI PROJECTS

Apple's CEO Tim Cook recently stated that the development of a self-driving car is the "mother of all AI projects." I agree with him wholeheartedly. He couldn't have said it any better. This is a succinct statement that says it all.

Some of you might question the boldness of the statement. On the surface, it seems like making a self-driving car is cut and dry. You hear every day about how we are on the verge of the self-driving car. If you believe that crock, I urge you to read about AI fake news on self-driving cars. We are a long ways away from having a true self-driving car. When I say a true one, I mean a Level 5 self-driving car. We are years and years away from achieving a Level 5 self-driving car, which essentially is a self-driving car that can drive in whatever manner that a human could drive a car.

This is a really, really, really hard thing to do.

Can you get a car that will drive along an open highway and pretty much act as a souped-up cruise control? Absolutely. We've got that right now in the Tesla and other upcoming "self-driving" cars. Can any of those cars take evasive action on their own initiative to avoid a car accident by realizing that there is a motorcyclist up ahead that is about to fall off his bike and land into traffic and therefore the self-driving car is wise enough to switch out its lane, doing so fully aware of the other traffic around it, and quickly go onto the shoulder? No.

This involves many aspects of human intelligence. This requires using judgment on-the-fly. It requires predicting the future. It requires preparing a plan of what to do. It requires carrying out the plan. It means adjusting the plan as the event evolves. It includes maneuvering the car suddenly and with care. It requires being aware of what the car is doing and trying to achieve. You could aim to program something for this particular scenario, but if you then vary the scenario the system would be unlikely to adjust to the new situation.

We need many more advances ahead of us to do this. We need advances in sensory devices. We need advances in the AI capabilities. Some of these advances we don't even know right now where they will arise from. Besides saying it is the mother of all AI projects, some liken this to being like a moonshot. Whenever someone refers to an innovation as a moonshot, they usually mean that it is something we can't do today, and for which we hope to do in the future, but how to get there is an open question that will require various miracle like breakthroughs to achieve.

That being said, let's do a step-by-step comparison to what a moonshot really was. In other words, let's retrace how we got to the moon, and see how those aspects are relevant to the creation of a true self-driving car and also how various factors differ from what we are doing for getting to a true self-driving car.

1. Big Stretch Goal

When it was proposed to go to the moon, no one really knew how we would get there. It was a big stretch goal. As Kennedy said, "We choose to go to the moon in this decade and do the other things, not because they are easy, but because they are hard."

Achieving a self-driving car is a big stretch goal, we don't yet know how to get there, and I would say: "We choose to develop a self-driving car and do other AI things, not because they are easy, but because they are hard."

2. Money Maker or Because-its-there

Going to the moon was not especially a money maker kind of engagement. It wasn't like we were going to cultivate the moon and start selling moon rocks and moon fruit to make money from the expedition. We wanted to go there to prove we could. It was bragging rights. It was pride.

Self-driving cars equals big bucks. It is the pot of gold at the end of this rainbow. I agree with the futurists that say it will transform society. This is big business. Now, I do agree that there are many other more altruistic reasons for having self-driving cars. But, really, for those firms putting in the time and effort right now, it's the money.

3. National Goal versus Private Goal

For the United States, getting to the moon was a national goal. It unified us. It gave us something to rally around. It allowed us to show that we were better than certain other countries.

There isn't a unified national goal around achieving a self-driving car. It's a mainly a private oriented goal. Car makers want to go there. Tech companies want to go there. The government is generally supportive of others that want to get there, but it is not fitting the whole bill and not taking an active role other than primarily as regulator.

4. It's a Race to Be First

The moonshot was a race. Who would get to the moon first? Turns out, it was pretty much a one-person race, in the end. A deadline had been established, get there by the end of the decade. We had a race and a finish line, along with a clear cut deadline.

For a self-driving car, there's a race by private firms to get there. Lots of participants in this race. It is assumed that whichever firm gets there first will grab up all the market share. Or at least be perceived as sterling and get lots of attention and boosted prices in their shares. There is not a known or stated deadline. No one knows how long it will really take. Some might tire of the race and drop out. Other new entrants might jump in. The finish line is somewhat nebulous in that though we could say it is whomever can achieve a Level 5 has reached the end, but we don't have a test per se to say what is really a Level 5 car and so the ending point is a bit murky.

5. Funding

The moonshot was mainly funded by the government. Which is funding from taxpayers.

Self-driving cars are funded by commercial ventures, by investors. Sure, there is some research done by universities and government funded, and government agencies doing research, but we're not going to see self-driving cars being produced by those entities. It's going to be commercial companies.

6. Public Excitement or Public Trepidation

So, the public was pretty excited about getting to the moon. It was a national rallying cry. Children in school knew to cheer for the astronauts and for every flight into space.

For self-driving cars, the public is keenly interested, but somewhat unsure and nervous. Will the self-driving cars be safe? Will they go berserk? Will they cost too much? Will the government try to control us by taking over our self-driving cars?

7. Technology Innovations

Getting to the moon required advances and innovations in technology. It helped spur the computer era that we know today and which benefited from immensely.

Some believe that for self-driving cars we already have the hardware we need. Elon Musk famously has claimed that the hardware on the latest Tesla's is sufficient for self-driving cars. This remains to be seen. The software side is a big question and so most would agree we don't have the AI part of this figured out. Elon thinks that once the AI part is figured out, he can just over-the-air pump the AI into the car and it will be a true self-driving car. We'll see. Anyway, I believe we need a lot of added technology innovations to get to a true self-driving car.

8. One-Time Achievement Versus Ongoing

Getting to the moon ended-up being a kind of one-time achievement. We got there. We walked around. We came back a few times.

A self-driving car is not the same in that we'll likely get a true self-driving car of capability X, and then want to evolve it to capability Y, and then to capability Z, etc. This is going to be an ongoing achievement.

9. Societal Impact Direct or Indirect

The moonshot had indirect impacts on society. It did not change the day-to-day lives of people. Some offshoots of the moonshot did ultimately change our lives, but the actual arriving at the moon did not. It might have created great spirit, which then led to other interests and later advances in technology. But the everyday person was not directly impacted by landing on the moon.

A self-driving car is going to change it all. All people will be directly impacted. Some say for example that it will change how the elderly live and what they can do. Some say it will change how we interact with each other. This is profound and transformative innovation.

10. Series of Steps Versus One Giant Leap

Getting to the moon took a series of painstaking steps. We first figured out how to get a rocket into outer space. We then took up monkeys. We then took up humans. We orbited the earth. We went to the moon but did not land. We finally then went to the moon and landed. It was not one giant leap overnight that got us there.

Self-driving cars are the same. We are going to get there one step at a time. That being said, some believe that we don't need to do this a step at a time. Rather than getting to Level 3, and then to Level 4, and then to Level 5, some say that the way to get there is to go from now to Level 5. Google's earlier plans were that way. They wanted to skip the intervening levels and get us to a Level 5. Doubtful about this. It is going to be more incremental than one giant leap.

11. Known by an Event Versus By Emergence

People remember where they were when we landed on the moon. It was a huge event. A life remembering event.

For a true self-driving car, I am doubtful that it will be that one day have some car maker that announces they have a Level 5 car and here it is. Voila. Take away the cape and there's a true self-driving car. Instead, it will emerge over time. There goes the Level 5 self-driving car, being tested again and again.

12. Things Will Go Wrong

You might know about Apollo 13, the mission that had to abort the moon mission and come back home. It was a success in that it proved that we could handle such an emergency. It was an example too of things that can go wrong. There were other notable setbacks too during the moon aiming years.

We have not yet had much go wrong per se on the path to self-driving cars. I am predicting that we will have lots go wrong (read my other books that cover product liability for self-driving cars). Nobody is speaking about it, but we are going to have accidents involving self-driving cars. We are going to have lawsuits. Just hope that it is doesn't curtail our enthusiasm and drive toward self-driving cars.

13. The New Norm

We had hoped that going to the moon would become a regular activity. People would live on the moon. Shuttles would go back-and-forth. Being there would be no different than living on Earth, other than the obvious precautions and living conditions differences. You would ride on a space rocket driven bus to get there and back. Hasn't happened yet.

For self-driving cars, it is intended to become the new norm. Once they are proven, eventually all cars will likely be self-driving cars. The only exceptions will be collector type of cars. The new norm will be self-driving cars.

14. Systems Intelligence

Getting to the moon required great skills in advancing computer hardware and software, but it was not AI. We didn't need systems that could act and "think" as humans can.

For a true self-driving car, we need intelligence on par with human intelligence. We need to get systems to behave as humans do. We can try to do this with black box approaches such as deep learning, or via white box approaches of programming the system, or a combination of the two. In any case, AI is a requirement. No AI, no self-driving cars.

The above covers some of the similarities and differences between a true moonshot and a true self-driving car in terms of being able to advance ourselves to achieve those aspects. The moonshot was the mother of all projects at the time.

Today, solving cancer is the mother of all medical projects (I realize some might argue that and claim it is some other medical malady). For AI, there are other AI achievements we are aiming to get to, but a self-driving car is definitely worthy of being consider the mother of them all.

In fact, I've stated many times that if we can do a self-driving car, it also means we can do AI at an incredible level that we can use that same AI for solving lots of other hard problems. Getting there is half the fun, and actually having a self-driving car that is truly a Level 5 will be a marvel of AI and mankind.

CHAPTER 12

MARKETING OF

SELF-DRIVING CARS

CHAPTER 12

MARKETING OF
SELF-DRIVING CARS

There is a popular car commercial that opens with a handsome man seated in a shiny new car and he is driving along the open highway. The wind is rushing and he has a big smile as he zips along in his sleek and speedy automobile. His hands are on the steering wheel. He's in control. Not a care in the world. He's on the open road and driving to who knows where, but it doesn't matter where he's driving to, he's driving. Music accompanies his ride and a helicopter view pans back to reveal his car taking this tight curve and another. He's wild. He's a beast. He's a manly man. Simply because he's driving that car.

Well, you'd think somehow a "manly man" would have to do some kind of manual labor like cutting down a tree or lifting tree stumps like a lumberjack. For driving a car, all you need to do is use one foot to press down on a pedal and a light touch on the steering wheel. Not much muscles needed for this. Where is the physical exertion?

Oops, sorry, didn't mean to take us away from the imagery of the car. Let's dive back into the commercial. The car comes up to a mansion. He drives up and there's a voluptuous stunning gorgeous woman standing there. She's his. Because of the car. Wow, that's some car. Any man would be crazy not to buy that car. You get to drive on the open roads, you get to go fast, you get the girl, and you get the mansion. I am rushing to go see my car dealer now.

Let's consider another car commercial. In this one, there's a woman driving the car. She is a harried mother and she's got two kids in the car. Though she's a harried mother, her makeup is impeccable and she looks like she is ready for a fashion show. She's pleasantly conversing with her children, giving them tips about life and living. How touching! One of the children is a young boy with a baseball cap and baseball uniform. Must be Little League or similar. The other child is a girl, wearing a delightful pink dress and ready for, not sure, maybe ballet? The three don't seem to have a care in the world and all is well.

All of a sudden, a kid on a skateboard is right in front of the car. The mother driving the car is caught by surprise. She starts to apply the brakes and fortunately this particular model of car has special emergency braking that takes over and ensures she does not plow into the kid. The car comes to a halt. She's OK, the children in the car are OK, and the jerk kid on the skateboard is OK. The mother looks affectionately at the car and approvingly seems to be saying to the car that it's a life saver. If she could kiss the car, she would. The camera pulls back and we see that now they are heading onward to their destination. Life is good. Once again, I need to rush out to my local dealership and get that car.

That's certainly what the car makers hope I will do. They market their cars in a manner that is intended to "inform" consumers about how great the cars are. It's more than just informational, of course. The marketers want to stir us to feel compelled to get the car. They must reach down inside our core and jog a primal instinct. Get the car. Get the car. It's a mantra conveyed in whatever manner will most cause us consumers to take action. Head down to the dealership, plunk down the cash, and buy that automobile.

How do the marketers and marketing efforts achieve this? It's not easy. As a consumer, you are bombarded by tons of advertisements and marketing campaigns. Buy this particular brand of toothpaste. Get your hair transplant here. Shop at this retail store. Go out and buy this model new car. These marketing messages come at you from all channels and at all hours. Radio, TV, cable, Internet ads, billboards, newspapers, you name it.

The minds of consumers need to be reached. Car marketing has a long history and has developed many successful aspects for inspiring people to buy cars. For getting males to buy a car, the typical marketing message is aimed at social status. As per the car commercial that I described earlier of the male driving the car, notice that it was all about being a manly man, and gaining social status. I might right now be a man that has no special social status, suppose I don't have a mansion, I am not able to drive the open roads because I work all week in a dinghy cubicle, and I don't have a gorgeous woman on my arm. How am I going to get those things? Why, by buying that new car. That's at least the "hidden" message of the car commercial.

That car commercial even uses a tag line of "be in the discerning few," which makes us apparently think that we're the only ones that can get that new car. By the way, that car is sold to thousands and thousands of people. Not especially a discerning few. Anyway, the marketers know how to push our buttons. They realize that our emotions will get us to buy that car. Our wants and desires are the forces that the marketing imagery needs to deeply tap into.

What about the other commercial, the one with the harried mother. In that case, the marketing is taking a different tack. The mother is saved by the car. It is like the classic story of the prince that saves the princess. For women, the marketers want to tap into the emotions and desires of being rescued, of being safe, of being saved. This car has those emergency brakes and it saved the life of the harried mother. Not just the mother, but it saved her children, and so it taps into the maternal instincts too.

It's not easy to cram into a 15 or 30 second commercial the kinds of marketing messages that you need to convey to sell a car. You might react to my above description of the two car commercials by becoming alarmed that both commercials are sexist. They rely upon clichés about what men are and what men want, and what women are and what women want.

Don't complain to me about this sexist viewpoint, it's what the car makers believe and hope will sell their cars. Indeed, there is lots of marketing research that shows these kinds of car commercials are actually very effective at doing so. I assure you that the car makers would not spend millions of dollars to produce the commercials, and then many millions more to air the commercials, if they didn't think they'd sell cars. I am not justifying what they are doing, and merely explaining it.

Marketers tend to divide the world into two types of personalities, those that are considered hedonic and versus those that are considered utilitarian.

The hedonics are seeking to fulfil promotion goals, they want to feel sophisticated, they want to be at a higher class. They seek fun. They want excitement in their lives. If you want them to buy a car or toothpaste or whatever, your messaging has to fit into that rooted way of living and thinking.

The utilitarian's have prevention oriented goals, they want to reduce the probability of things going badly. They seek safety. They seek security. They want to feel smart and appear like they are a responsible shopper. If you want them to buy a car or toothpaste or whatever, your messaging has to fit into that rooted way of living and thinking.

For men, usually the hedonic approach of selling a car is best. Appeal to their desire for excitement and social class. Show them that the car will get them those things. For women, the utilitarian approach of selling a car is usually best. Aim at the safety aspects, such as avoiding hitting a kid on a skateboard. Demonstrate that the car will keep them and others that are around them safe.

Now, I realize some of you are saying that you are a man but that the utilitarian approach is more fitting, or you are a woman and you think the hedonic is a better fit for you. That's great. Everyone is different. Marketers though need to think about the numbers, and aim at the largest audience they can. If most men are a certain way X, within the target market, then the marketing needs to aim that way. Likewise, if most women are a certain way Y, within the target market, then the marketing needs to aim that way. Sure, there will be exceptions, but if you only have the budget to make one commercial you need to go for the segment that has the bigger chance of being swayed.

One of the advantages of marketing via the Internet is that a marketer can tailor the marketing message in a very specific way. A television commercial is aimed broadly. An insert of a short video clip on the Internet can be based on whatever is known about the Internet viewer. If you are age 18 and a male, a video that has just the right marketing message can be aimed at you. If you are a 32-year-old female and you are known to be buying diapers, a different video message can be aimed at you. The medium or channel can allow for offering tailored messaging.

Now that I've dragged you through a core class in marketing, you might wonder why I am doing so.

Here at the Cybernetic Self-Driving Car Institute, we are studying and getting ready for the changes in marketing of cars to consumers once the advent of self-driving cars actually hits the roads.

You might be thinking that the selling of cars shouldn't make a difference as to whether the car is a regular conventional human driven car versus a self-driving car. You'd be wrong.

We'll start by discussing the true self-driving car, a self-driving car at the Level 5 (see my article about the Richter scale of self-driving cars). A Level 5 self-driving car is one that involves no human intervention. The AI and automation entirely is able to drive the car. You don't need to touch a steering wheel and nor put a foot onto a pedal. The car drives itself. You tell it where you want to go, and it takes you there. No effort per se on your part. Humans not needed, other than to be an occupant of the car.

Let's now revisit the two car commercials that I discussed at the start of this piece. The first commercial had a man driving the car, while the second commercial had a woman driving the car. Guess what, there isn't any human driving a true Level 5 car. If the man is not going to be driving the car, it makes no sense to have a car commercial that tries to convey them as being manly because they are driving the car. They aren't driving the car anymore. Yikes! Driving the car is

141

nearly what every car commercial today shows.

What will you show if there isn't a human driving the car? That's the marketing million-dollar question. You can no longer appeal to that hidden desire of being the manly man, or the caring maternal mother, by showing the man or the woman driving the car. This is tough. The whole concept is that the driver of the car is in control. Not anymore. The AI and automation is essentially in control. The man and the woman are now merely occupants.

Suppose you say that we'll still put that man into the self-driving car, and they are shown in a commanding way because they order the car to take them to the mansion where the gorgeous woman awaits. I am sure that some marketers will try this, but I doubt it will be very successful. Somehow it does not seem compelling to just be sitting in the self-driving car and barking out orders.

There are some other ways though to approach this.

When true self-driving cars first appear, the marketers can make it seem like any man that has that kind of car is more socially prominent than men that are driving the old-fashioned ways.

Imagine this as the car commercial of the future. A man gets into his self-driving car, and a gorgeous woman is already in there. He and she eye each other coyly. The man turns to the AI at the front of the car and says to take them to the chateau. The two begin to share a bottle of champagne. The door closes and the self-driving car starts to drive off. What's happening in that self-driving car? I think you know.

Which would you rather be, the man driving a car that is going to meet a gorgeous woman, or the man in a car that has a gorgeous woman and the two of them are maybe already doing some hanky panky. I am betting the hanky panky version will be more compelling.

The point is that we'll still be able to use the hedonic approach and the utilitarian approach, but will just need to shift somewhat to accommodate the aspect that the car is a self-driving car. People will still be people. The car is different, but the messaging related to the inner drive of people remains the same.

For the utilitarian messaging, it can shift somewhat to accommodate the self-driving car. Right now, we have messaging about the fuel efficiency of cars, trying to get you to buy a car that is not a gas guzzler. This is a utilitarian aim. By the time that we have many self-driving cars, they probably will be pretty much all electric based cars, and so the fuel efficiency issue will no longer loom particularly.

Performance of cars will still be on the table. A sports car will still be a sports car, and messaging about how fast it goes and that it can zoom from zero to 60 miles per hour is still applicable. What is different though is that the occupants aren't driving the car. It makes things harder to appeal to the speed of the car when there is not a human driver. Will people be excited to be in a sports car that can go fast, but that it is the AI that is driving the car? We'll have to see. I remember that at Disneyland they used to have People Movers, which were kind of "cars" that you rode in, and some would go fast and others slow. The ones that went fast, those appealed to certain personalities. Maybe in the real-world it will work the same way.

Currently, in the United States there is about four billion dollars spent on automobile advertising. Some are saying that once we have self-driving cars that the amount of spending on marketing those cars will drop tremendously. Those pundits seem to think that all self-driving cars will be the same and so a consumer will not be prodded toward buying one versus another. I say that's a crock.

We will continue to have cars that are distinctive of each other, in spite of them being self-driving cars. You can still have an SUV versus a sports car. You can still have a car that has a particular shape and social status to it. We are not going to be riding in one-size-fits-all cars that are self-driving cars. This just doesn't make much sense. Those living in this kind of utopian dream world are wacky. In the real-world, there will be car makers, car brands, models of cars, and so on.

That being said, there will also be differences in other ways that are specific to being a self-driving car. For example, when self-driving cars start appearing, they will have little of any track records. Therefore, the self-driving car makers will try to showcase that their self-driving car has been better tested than another. We're the Widget maker of the self-driving car Quickzo, and our Quickzo has been tested on forty million miles of driving for the last two years. It's the safest and best tested self-driving car out there. That's the early kind of self-driving car commercials we'll likely see.

In fact, here's what we'll see:

- Comparing self-driving cars to conventional human driven cars (showcasing how much easier, better, etc. the self-driving car is).

- Meanwhile conventional human driven cars will market that why give up control when you can still be in control of your own car (and try to keep defections of those eyeing self-driving cars).

- Some car makers will try to convince you that you need a second or third car, of which it should be a self-driving car, and yet you can still keep around your old-fashioned conventional car. Be at the front of the pack and have a self-driving car on your driveway.

- Makers of human driven cars will be somewhat in a bind if they try to highlight the dangers of self-driving cars, since they too are likely going to be edging into the self-driving car market and don't want to ruin that future market by poisoning consumers about it.

- During early days of having choices among different self-driving cars by differing car makers, it will be a features war of which self-driving car has more AI automation than another.

Those pundits that are trying to predict the marketing future of self-driving cars are often also missing the boat on another important element about marketing. Namely that the consumer marketplace will evolve over time, and that there will be the classic adoption cycle involved.

The classic adoption cycle is that any new innovation tends to be adopted by waves of consumers. The initial and smallest part of the consumer market is the Innovators, usually comprising about 2% of the adopters. Next, the Early Adopters come along, wanting to try what the brave souls of the Innovators have now already been trying out, and this about 14% of the adopters. You then have the Early Majority, which is around 34% of the adopters. Followed by the Late Majority, at about 34% of the market. And ending with the Laggards, at 16% of the market. Those Laggards are the ones least likely to embrace the innovation, if ever.

The marketing messages to each of these segments needs to be aimed at that particular segment. In other words, how you appeal to the Innovators is different than how you appeal to the Late Majority, for example. The Innovators want to get the latest hot new toy. Indeed, one could argue that most of the sales to-date of the Tesla's have been to the Innovators segment of the market. With the next Tesla 3 coming out, we'll see if the Tesla brand can appeal to a much wider audience and tap into a larger base of Innovators and/or Early Adopters.

For anyone wanting to be the first at marketing of self-driving cars, be aware that the self-driving cars market will not happen overnight. It will emerge over several years. Self-driving cars will gradually come to the market. It won't be an overnight sensation like a sudden pet rock that appears and grabs a hold of the market. Furthermore, consumers will not just abandon their conventional cars and instantly switch to self-driving cars. We'll be seeing the market staggered among the Innovators, Early Adopter, Early Majority, Late Majority, and Laggards, occurring over several years.

It will be an exciting time for car makers as they try to reach both conventional human driver car markets and the self-driving car markets. In the far future, we'll eventually see less and less of conventional human driven cars, but I assure you it's a long ways off in the future. The base of some 200 million estimated existing conventional cars is not going to disappear overnight. The dual messaging about being a human driver will remain for a while. Get out your marketing ideas and be ready to help those self-driving car makers figure out how to best move those self-driving cars off the lots. At first, it will be pretty easy and the marketing is going to be easy too. After competition picks up, it will be the usual marketing battle of hand-to-hand combat to sell your self-driving car over someone else's. I'm looking forward to that day!

.

CHAPTER 13

ARE AIRPLANE AUTOPILOT SYSTEMS THE SAME AS SELF-DRIVING CAR AI

CHAPTER 13

ARE AIRPLANE AUTOPILOT SYSTEMS THE SAME AS SELF-DRIVING CAR AI

As a frequent speaker at AI automated vehicle and self-driving car conferences, and as Executive Director at the Cybernetic Self-Driving Car Institute, I often get asked about the nature of airplane autopilot systems and how they compare to what is going on with self-driving car AI systems. I like the questions since it gives me a chance to explain the similarities and differences between the two, plus it also provides an opportunity to burst some bubbles about the myths associated with both.

Here's the types of questions that I get asked, and for which I will answer herein:

- Is an airplane autopilot the same as a self-driving car AI system?

- Can't we just clone an airplane autopilot and use it to have ourselves a self-driving car?

- Flying a plane takes years of training and experience, so certainly the airplane autopilot must be many times more sophisticated than what is needed for a self-driving car?

- Anybody can drive a car, so it must be much easier to develop AI for a self-driving car than it is for an airplane?

Let's take a look at these questions and figure out what's what.

First, let's begin by reviewing what an airplane autopilot system does. There are a number of myths involved and the public perception is a far cry from the reality of what plane automation actually achieves.

A plane has various sensors around the plane to help gauge the speed of the airplane, its altitude, and other flight related factors. You could say this is somewhat similar to the need for sensors on a self-driving car (see my article about sensor fusion on self-driving cars).

A self-driving car has perhaps radar, LIDAR (see my article about LIDAR), cameras, ultrasonic sensors, and other various sensory devices around it. Airplane sensors collect data during the flight of the plane, as likewise the sensors of the self-driving car collect data during a driving journey. So far, they seem pretty much alike, a plane and a self-driving car. Planes do though have some different sensors than a self-driving car, and indeed a self-driving car has some sensors that are not normally included on a plane, but we'll ignore that difference and just gentlemanly agree that both have sensors to collect important data while underway. That seems fair.

The sensory data is collected and computer processors do sensor fusion, using the sensory data for purposes of guiding and controlling the plane and likewise the same for a self-driving car. In a self-driving car, there is a need to control the accelerator and brake pedals, the steering wheel, and the like, thus directing the car. Similarly, the airplane autopilot needs to be able to control and direct the plane, adjusting its direction, altitude, speed, etc. Once again, it seems like the two are about the same.

Currently, even if there is an airplane autopilot available on a plane, a pilot or flight certified crew member must be present in the cockpit at all times. The human pilot is considered ultimately responsible for the operation of the plane. This is equally true for Levels 1 to Level 4 for a self-driving car (see my article on the Richter scale for self-driving cars). For those levels of self-driving cars, there must be a human driver present and the human driver must be properly qualified to drive the car. The human driver needs to be ready to intervene if the self-driving car AI asks them to do so, or if the human driver perceives the need to take over the controls from the self-driving car.

Now, for a Level 5 self-driving car, the rules change. A true self-driving car is a Level 5, which is a self-driving car that can entirely drive itself and there isn't ever any human intervention needed. Simply stated, it is not necessary to have a human driver available. There is no equivalent right now for airplanes. Airplanes are considered always to be watched by a human pilot.

Will we someday change that rule? Maybe, but it will probably be much later than after we have Level 5 self-driving cars. The reason perhaps is that flying a plane that has 300 passengers is considered a much more serious task than someone being in a car with a single occupant or a few more. We will likely for a long time continue to insist that a human pilot needs to be ready to take over the controls of an airplane autopilot, right or wrong in our perception of what the airplane autopilot can or cannot do.

Things start to get more interesting as we move further into the details about what an airplane autopilot currently does.

Let's begin by identifying what steps occur when we want to have a plane take us on a flight. Normally, the plane is parked at a terminal, and it needs to somehow move away from the terminal and taxi to a runway position where it can be ready to takeoff, once at that position it needs to takeoff from the ground and get airborne. Once airborne, the plane needs to climb up in the air and reach a desired altitude. After achieving a desired altitude, the airplane will usually stay at the altitude for a period of time and be considered at a cruising or level flight position. Eventually, the plane will need to start to descend. Once the descent has reached a low enough position and the plane is near a runway, the plane is taken into its approach. At the conclusion of the approach is the landing of the plane, and it then usually needs to taxi to a place where it will be parked.

In recap: Taxi -> Takeoff -> Climb -> Cruise -> Descend -> Approach -> Land -> Taxi.

Today's airplane autopilots rarely ever do the taxiing and it is expected that the human pilot will do so. This is kind of interesting because of course a self-driving car is all about "taxiing" in that the self-driving car must drive on a road and be able to do so without human intervention for Level 5 cars. Some say that after we've perfected self-driving cars, we should port over the same AI capability to airplanes.

Most airplane autopilots are not able to land the plane, and those that do have such a landing capability are rarely used. Normally, a human pilot will land the plane. The exceptions are typically under very adverse weather conditions. This at first seems counter-intuitive since you would assume that the automation would do the easy flight landings and you'd only have the human handle the tricky landings involving bad weather. The reason that the autopilot might be used for bad weather is that it has instruments or sensors that can tell it things that the human pilot cannot necessarily as readily ascertain by looking outside the plane and by looking at the gauges. This though is a judgment call and I'd wager that most experienced pilots would rather be at the controls over using the autopilot in the adverse weather conditions.

Let's now review what the airplane autopilot situation is:

Taxi: Not today
Takeoff: Can do, but rare
Climb: Can do, but rare
Cruise: Most usage
Descend: Can do, but rare
Approach: Can do, but rare
Land: Can do, but very very seldom
Taxi: Not today

In essence, the bulk of the use of an airplane autopilot is when the plane is cruising along at level flight. When you have nearly anything else happening, the human pilot takes over the controls. Even at cruising flight the human pilot might take over if there is a lot of turbulence or anything out of the ordinary happening.

I know that many movies and the public perception is that a human pilot pretty much sits back and simply lets the autopilot fly the plane from end-to-end of a flight journey, but this is a myth. Another myth is that even once the autopilot is engaged during the cruising part of the flight that the pilot is reading a newspaper or otherwise doing something that allows them to be completely unobservant about the plane status. This is considered a forbidden aspect and it is fully expected that the human pilot must be always aware of the status of the plane and be instantly ready to take over the controls.

In theory, the same is true for the self-driving cars at levels 1 to 4. Though some people falsely think that at those levels the human driver can be playing cards, it is not what the definition indicates. The human driver is still responsible for the car. The human driver must be ready to intervene in the driving task. The only viable way to be able to intervene involves paying attention to the driving journey and the status of the self-driving car. We won't be able to sit back and read the newspaper until we are making use of Level 5 self-driving cars, which is still a ways ahead in the future.

In fact, anyone that knows anything about airplane autopilots always says this: The airplane autopilot does not fly the plane, the human pilot is flying the plane via the use of automation.

Notice that an important distinction is that the human pilot is always flying the plane, and he or she is merely using automation to assist. You need to think of levels 1 to 4 of self-driving cars the same way. It is the human driver that is driving the car and using automation to do much of the driving task. Only once you get to level 5 can you then say that it is no longer the human driving the car, and instead it becomes the automation driving the car.

The airplane autopilot is mainly intended today for handling long stretches of a flight that are somewhat boring. Nothing unusual should be happening. In one sense, this is handy for a human pilot because they might become overly bored themselves during long stretches and begin to mishandle the plane. By allowing the autopilot to deal with the monotony, you pretty much know that the automation can remain alert and steady. This is good.

Of course, what can be bad involves situations when a plane that is cruising for a long stretch and suddenly out-of-the-blue has an unexpected emergency. It can be tough for the human pilot to instantly re-engage in the flight. Many of the most famous flight crashes while cruising are due to the Human-Machine Interface (HMI) issues of when a plane startlingly asks the human pilot to intervene. It is easy for a human pilot to become inadvertently complacent during a long and mundane stretch of a cruise.

Pilots that I know are often upset to hear the public say things like an autopilot is better than the human pilot, or that the autopilot flies the plane entirely and the human pilot is nothing more than an overpaid glorified baby sitter for the automation. If you want to get a human pilot really angry, go ahead and say this to their face. Dare you.

In fact, pilots often prefer to refer to the autopilot as an auto flight system. They think that by using the word "pilot" in autopilot that it misleads the public into believing that the automation is more far reaching than it really is. I would argue that most autopilot systems aren't even much in terms of AI. We've had the basics of autopilots for many years. These autopilot systems predate the latest advances in AI. Few of the more complex AI capabilities are currently involved in autopilots.

Tesla has gotten itself into some hot water by deciding to call their self-driving car capabilities an "Autopilot" (I'll capitalize it to distinguish the brand name from the common use of the word). Elon Musk seems to think that the phrasing of Autopilot is apt because he wants people to leverage their myth-like understanding of airplane autopilots into assuming that his Tesla cars are equally as impressive in their automation. There have been various agencies and governments that have wanted to get Tesla to change the name of their automation, because it is felt that the Autopilot is a misleading moniker.

I've already predicted in my articles about product liability in self-driving cars that Tesla might eventually regret having used the Autopilot naming. At some point, once more self-driving car crashes happen, and I'm not saying that Tesla will be alone in having car crashes (since all self-driving car makers will have them once we have more self-driving cars on the roads), once there are more crashes of Tesla's, someone harmed or killed is going to have a family member press the case that Tesla misled the public about what the automation could do. As evidence, the family could try to show that the word Autopilot and autopilot are purposely intended to confuse and mislead buyers and drivers of the Tesla's. Don't know whether they can make that case stick, but I am sure that some lawyers will try.

For human pilots of airplanes, they affectionally refer to autopilot systems often as "George" and it is a kind of wink-wink pet name. They know that the autopilot is rarely even one system, and instead a collection of several subsystems. The human pilot tends to act like an orchestra conductor and make sure that each subsystem is doing what it is intended to do. An analogy sometimes used by pilots is that they are like brain surgeons in a highly advanced and automated surgical operating room. The human medical doctor is still doing the operation, even if they might have highly sophisticated microscopes and biological cutting tools.

There are AI proponents that feel like pilots are trying to keep their head in the sand and refusing to accept that airplane autopilot technology could be better. Or, some cynically say that the pilot unions are worried about job losses of pilots. The unions supposedly would prefer that an autopilot not be able to completely handle a plane from end-to-end. Imagine the massive layoffs of pilots and that we might eventually lose the skill to manually fly planes. That's a future doom and gloom picture that is often portrayed.

In terms of cloning an airplane autopilot for purposes of aiding self-driving cars AI, the answer there is that it is not particularly the case that we can get much from doing so. As mentioned, the autopilot generally handles the cruising aspects of the plane. Today's self-driving cars are somewhat doing the same thing, in that most of the current self-driving cars are only able to do cruising down an open highway. They are simply doing tricks of following lane markings and the car ahead of them. Anything out of the ordinary requires human intervention. The plane autopilot and today's self-driving cars match on that sense of simplicity of the ability to control the vehicle.

One would say that the plane is even less complex an environment than what faces a self-driving car. Sure, an instrumental panel on a plane is baffling and overwhelming to anyone not familiar with flying, but keep in mind that planes are somewhat traveling like a train. A train has train tracks that force it to go certain ways. In the skies, for most flying and especially cruising, there are defined lanes in the sky. A plane is given coordinates to fly in a certain direction at a certain speed, and the air traffic controller tries to ensure that no other plane is in that same path.

When you drive your car, you aren't given the same kind of clear path for where your car goes and what other cars around you are doing. A plane is normally steering clear of another plane, doing so as guided by the air traffic controllers. Cars are in a free-for-all most of the time. Yes, I realize that we have lanes on freeways, but there isn't anything or anyone telling that car next to you to stay back from your car, or opening up the lane to let you make a lane change. How many times do planes crash into each other? It's very rare. When it happens, there is a big news blitz, and so maybe you think it happens all the time, but it is actually very rare. Cars crash all the time.

Cars are faced with motorcyclists that can come within inches of your car. Pedestrians can jump in the front of your car. Kids can throw bricks off an overpass and the projectile can smash into your front windshield. Your tire can go over a nail and get punctured, with rapid and sudden loss of steering control of your car due to a flattened tire. On and on. Though things can go awry on planes, they are generally carefully maintained and they are flown away from areas that could harm the plane. We've all heard about the occasions when birds got sucked into a plane engine and a plane had to make an emergency landing, but these are rare and memorable because they are rare.

In the above manner, developing AI for a self-driving car is much harder right now than for an airplane autopilot. I know that some flight software developers will get irked at this statement, and so let me qualify it. If we want an airplane to be more like a Level 5 true self-driving car, we definitely have an uphill battle of creating software for planes that is that good. Having an autopilot that could do everything a human pilot might do, and cover all the permutations of things that any plane can encounter, this is a very hard problem, I agree.

Human pilots require extensive training and experience so that when the 1% of the time something goes awry, they are ready. They need to save their lives and the lives of the 300 passengers on the plane. For cars, we put teenagers through some pretty slim training and then toss them onto our roads. Heaven help us. They though eventually seem to figure it out, and we are not overly beset with teenage mutant driver killers.

One aspect of autopilots that I really like is that the autopilot hardware and software is extensively designed and built for redundancy and resiliency. You often have multiple redundant hardware processors on planes, allowing one processor to take over if another one falters. You have redundant software such as for the Space Shuttle that was developed with multiple versions, and each version double-checks the other. Few of the self-driving car makers are doing this.

Self-driving car makers are not being as rigorous as those that have developed autopilot systems. This is kind of crazy since self-driving cars are going to be immersed in places and situations of greater complexity than what autopilots do of today.

I realize that the thinking is that if an autopilot falters that then a plane falls out of the sky, while if a self-driving car AI falters it is not going to fall from the sky, plus the human driver can just take over the controls. Keeping in mind that we are heading to Level 5 self-driving cars, we will need AI systems that have the rigors of what we expect for plane autopilots.

I hope this discussion about airplane autopilots and the AI of self-driving cars is helpful to you, and maybe when a friend or even a stranger asks you the questions about the similarities and differences, you'll now be ready to answer their questions.

By the way, we don't yet have a pet-like name for self-driving car AI, recall I mentioned that autopilots are often referred to as George by insiders. I think we need to have a contest to determine a catchy insider name for self-driving car AI. I'll start the voting, and offer that we either call it Michael or Lauren.

CHAPTER 14

SAVVY SELF-DRIVING CAR REGULATORS: ASSEMBLYMAN MARC BERMAN

CHAPTER 14

SAVVY SELF-DRIVING CAR REGULATORS ASSEMBLYMAN MARC BERMAN

I recently served on a panel of speakers at a self-driving car event in Silicon Valley and met a fellow panelist, Assemblyman Marc Berman, known for his savvy awareness about self-driving cars. During the panel, Marc offered numerous insights that showcased his prowess in understanding the nature of where self-driving cars are today and where they are heading. His kind of expertise about self-driving cars is sorely needed by our regulators at all of the state, federal, and local levels.

This new innovation of self-driving cars will either be helped or possibly hampered by regulations and so somehow regulators need to get up-to-speed akin to what this Assemblyman representing the 24th District in California is doing (his district covers essentially the heart of Silicon Valley, including Palo Alto, Sunnyvale, and parts of Santa Clara county and San Mateo County). You might want to take a look at his TEDx talk that he gave on driverless cars back in February 2013. He's been thinking about self-driving cars for a while and has his fingers on the pulse of the ways in which driverless cars will impact our society.

Indeed, Assemblyman Berman has launched an initiative entitled "Silicon Valley 2028" that includes enabling the safe deployment of self-driving cars. He is urging his fellow legislators to aid in the development of a comprehensive legal framework covering self-driving cars. There are many upcoming legal issues that will emerge as self-driving cars begin to actually appear on our roadways. Right now, the laws about self-driving cars are patchy at best. Self-driving car makers are in fact worried that what might be legal for a self-driving car in one state might turn out to be illegal in another state. This would be problematic for the selling of self-driving cars and for consumers that want to buy self-driving cars and drive them from one state to the next.

Imagine that you were driving your car today to go from say California to Nevada (it's a popular driving effort for those in Southern California that favor visiting Las Vegas and trying their hands at the betting tables). Suppose that California driving laws stated that you had to drive a certain way, and suppose further that Nevada laws indicated you had to drive in a different manner in terms of rules-of-the-road. It would be difficult for you as the driver to make sure that you switched over to the rules of Nevada when you crossed the state border line. This is the same aspect that we might face with self-driving cars. If each state decides to go in a particular direction on what they expect a self-driving car to do, the myriad of disparate regulations can make life arduous for both the makers of the self-driving cars and for those that buy one and want to travel from state to state.

Now, when I've mentioned this concern about the state-to-state disparity on self-driving car regulations, I've had some techies that instantly retort that the beauty of a self-driving car is that it should presumably be easily reprogrammable such that it can adapt to multiple regulations. In other words, the AI should be setup to have a module that knows about the driving regulations in California. Once it reaches Nevada, it should simply swap out the California module and then plug in the Nevada module. This might be akin to having two human drivers in a conventional car and having one that is licensed to drive in California and one that is licensed to drive in Nevada. Each takes the driver's wheel when in the state for which they are licensed to drive.

Yes, I realize that this notion of modules for driving within states is certainly feasible. But, what is missing from that discussion is that suppose one state says that a self-driving car can use LIDAR, and another state bans its use. If the self-driving car you are in happens to use LIDAR, and it goes into another state that has banned it, the self-driving car might possibly now be partially blind to the roadway. I am not saying that any state currently has made such a ban, but merely pointing out that the regulations in a given state could be of an onerous nature that it would possibly cripple or undermine a self-driving car that is readily allowed to drive in another state.

I am an adviser to the U.S. congressman that serves as Vice Chair on the congressional science and technology committee and so I try to keep well-informed of what the feds and the states are doing in terms of technology related regulations. Recently, the Senate Committee on commerce, science, and transportation had a hearing on the topic of self-driving cars. Testimony by several industry notables kept coming back to the suggestion that a single, unified national standard for self-driving car regulations is needed.

For example, currently each state is establishing its own policies and procedures on the testing of self-driving cars. Some states don't have any stated policies and procedures. States that do have on-the-books policies and procedures have at times crafted those regulations from scratch and so the regulations are not as robust as they could be. Besides the regulations varying from state to state, there are at times provisions in one that are not found in another. Some critics say it is the wild, wild west right now in terms of what self-driving car makers can and cannot do, within each state, and this makes it more costly and confounding to be an innovator trying to make self-driving cars.

Safety guidelines are probably the most important of the regulations that are to be passed. In the state of Washington, they recently passed new regulations about self-driving cars. One aspect that registered some controversy involved the indication that there does not need to be a human driver ready to take over from the AI of the self-driving cars that are being tested on the public roadways of Washington.

Critics liken this looseness and the aspect that Washington has formed a state-wide committee to further study the matter as similar to what Arizona established in 2015. Critics say that Arizona has been overly lax in their regulations, meanwhile Arizona has attracted many of the self-driving car makers due to the less-is-more mindset of having minimal regulatory hurdles on self-driving cars.

If you look closely at the Executive Order 17-02 "Autonomous Vehicle Testing & Technology in Washington State" you'll see that it offers two different kinds of allowed pilot programs of self-driving car testing. One pilot program involves the "safe testing and operation of autonomous vehicles with human operators present" and requires that the vehicle needs to be monitored and operation "only by a trained employee, contractor, or other person authorized by the entity developing autonomous technology." Furthermore, the human operator must have a valid U.S. driver's license and the vehicle owner must provide proof of financial responsibility of the car. This is similar to the self-driving car regulations in California.

The other pilot program in the Washington law involves "autonomous vehicles without human operators present," which is the controversial element of the Washington state law. This pilot program says that "vehicles shall be equipped with an automated driving system that performs all aspects of the driving task on a part- or full-time basis within the vehicle's operational design limits, and it must be capable of bringing the vehicle to safe condition in the event of a system failure." You might recognize this language as being similar to the Society for Automotive Engineers (SAE) provisions for the levels of self-driving cars.

The reason that there are opponents of this second type of allowed pilot program is that it presumably means that we'll have self-driving cars being tested on the public roads of Washington and yet not need to have a human operator ready to intervene when needed. In the levels of self-driving cars, it is only the true self-driving car of Level 5 that indicates no human driver is needed and that the car must be able to drive in whatever manner a human driver can drive. We are still a long ways away from having a Level 5 self-driving car. Furthermore, notice that the provision says "part- or full-time basis" which implies that the self-driving car does not need to be full-time devoted to the driving task of the car. What will happen when the self-driving car reaches a point of not knowing what to do and tries to hand the controls over to a presumed human operator?

Further criticism is aimed at the provision because it says that "developing entities shall self-certify to the DOL [Department of Licensing] that they are compliant." Notice that it says that the self-driving car maker is able to self-certify. This implies that the state government is not going to do the certification itself to ensure that the self-driving car can safety operator without a human operator present. Those critical of this provision are saying that it is allowing the wolf to say it is safe to be amongst the sheep. Governor Jay Inslee of the state of Washington has indicated that he wanted purposely to allow for having a "relatively light touch" with regulations imposed upon the self-driving car industry.

Assemblyman Marc Berman in his remarks on the panel that he and I served on expressed rightfully that there needs to be a balance between having too few regulatory requirements and too many. He has called for self-driving car stakeholders to come together and derive consistent and workable regulations. This is a welcomed outreach.

If we have too few regulations it could lead to regrettably life threatening or even death producing situations during this pioneering era of the self-driving car emergence. The result could be a stampede toward shutting down the self-driving car parade. We could end-up seeing self-driving car innovations come nearly to a halt and the progress hindered for years to come. At the same time, if regulations are overly restrictive at this time, it could stunt the innovation before it gets a chance to get off the ground. We need the proverbial "Goldilocks" set of legal provisions, ones that are just right, and they need to be adopted across the board at state, federal, and local levels.

Many regulators seem to think only in terms of one end of the spectrum or another. There are either a thousand pages of regulations needed and every time bit of legal ground needs to be covered, or there is a one page regulation that leaves wide open interpretation that can produce high safety risks. These extremes aren't a good way to go on this. All it will take is one bad apple of a particular self-driving car maker that happens to put a car onto the roadway that kills someone in a jurisdiction that allowed for a wide-open landscape, and then all the other states and the feds will be (forced) to step into this like a ton of bricks. Before we get to that unfortunate and undesirable juncture, it would be better to identify and codify an appropriate balance and put regulations onto the books that we can all satisfactorily live with.

As mentioned at the start of this chapter, we need more regulators like Assemblyman Marc Berman. In my role as the Executive Director of the Cybernetic Self-Driving Car Institute, I urge regulators from other states that are desirous of a fellow informed legislator, one that they can brainstorm with about this topic, they should give him a call. His being based in Silicon Valley partially derives his penchant for new technology like self-driving cars. That being the case, it makes sense to leverage his expertise and passion for this topic. If Silicon Valley can be the generator of AI and innovations for making self-driving cars, it can also be the innovator and guiding light as to what self-driving car regulations should be like too.

.

CHAPTER 15

EVENT DATA RECORDERS (EDR'S) FOR SELF-DRIVING CARS

CHAPTER 15

EVENT DATA RECORDERS (EDR'S) FOR SELF-DRIVING CARS

By now, we all are generally aware that airplanes often have a so-called "black box" that is intended to survive flight crashes and be used to retrieve essential information about what happened during the flight. There are sometimes more than one such device, each being focused on a particular aspect of a flight. For example, one black box to capture the flight controls data such as speed and altitude, while another black box is used to capture sounds inside the cockpit of the plane to record what the crew was talking about.

In most cases, the black boxes run on the basis of recording information for a set number of minutes and then write over that recording as new information comes in. Let's say that a black box had the capacity to record 15 minutes' worth of information. It would start recording at the beginning of the flight, and when the first fifteen minutes were past, it would get rid of the first recorded minute by overwriting it with the 16th minute, then get rid of the second minute of recording with the 17th minute, and so on. This provides a window of just 15 minutes of what took place, based on any current instant in time. If a plane crash actually took 20 minutes to occur, and if we assume that the black box stopped recording once the plane hit the ground, we would only know about the last fifteen minutes of the flight and not have data prior to that point in time (we would not know what occurred in the first 5 minutes of this 20 minute long crash scenario).

There are some black boxes that don't record anything until the point at which they are triggered to operate. Returning to the scenario about the plane crash, it might be that the black box did not start doing any recording at the beginning of the flight. Instead, when the flight begins to exhibit a problem, it might trigger the black box to operate. Suppose that the right engine of the plane suddenly stops working. This might be a preset trigger to start the black box. The black box then does its recordings. If it has a limited data volume, let's pretend it only can hold five minutes' worth of data, it would then have the last five minutes of the flight, assuming too that it stops recording once it hits the ground. At times, the black box might not realize that it hit the ground per se, and so might continue recording even after the crash is completed (which, again, if there is a limited capacity to the black box, could mean that valuable info about the ending of the crash could be lost).

Why all this discussion about black boxes? Because we are going to become increasing reliant on them for self-driving cars, at least that's one viewpoint, which, as you'll see next, carries some controversy to it.

At the Cybernetic Self-Driving Car Institute, we are keenly interested in black boxes for cars. They potentially hold the key to understanding what happened in the case of a self-driving car that gets into a crash. Allow me to elaborate.

First, instead of referring to them as black boxes (nowadays they are at times varying in colors, for example orange is a popular color so that it can stand out amongst crash rubble), we call them Event Data Recorders (EDR).

Believe it or not, EDR's or black boxes for cars have been around for a while (it's not a new idea to use a black box that normally is used on an airplane to also put one into a car). During the mid-1990s, several prominent car makers opted to start including EDR's, such as in Pontiacs and Buicks. There was little fanfare about this. Consumers were pretty much unaware of the inclusion of an EDR into their car. It's not the kind of added feature that car manufactures tout, which makes sense to avoid mentioning because it otherwise brings up the unpleasant notion that someday your car might crash and you'll be killed in it. But, hey, at least the EDR will survive! That's not a stirring reason to rush out to buy a particular brand of car that is equipped with a black box.

Why are they so prominent on airplanes? I think we can all pretty much agree that having a black box for an airplane is something we, the public, believe is for the good of the public. When a plane crashes, and suppose it holds 300 souls, a lot of family members and regulators want to know why that plane went down. If there are no survivors, we have no particular information about what happened on the flight. Even if there are survivors, they might not know what happened. Even if the pilot or co-pilot survives, they might not know, or might misremember, or might (rarely) even lie about what happened.

Not only is the black box handy for understanding a particular crash, it also is helpful for the plane makers. Suppose the black box recording reveals that a model of airplane cannot handle severe rain at high altitudes due to what is found to be a design limitation in the wings of the plane. This would allow the plane manufacturer to redesign the wings accordingly. Or, suppose the plane had problems due to the tail of the plane, and we later found out that the tail was not getting the prescribed monthly maintenance, this would help to guide that all such planes need to rigorously get their needed monthly maintenance.

In short, the black box on a plane helps to understand what occurred during a crash, it can lead to improvements in how planes are designed and made, it can lead to improvements about how planes are maintained. There is also another set of important reasons. Families of those killed in a plane crash want to know whether the plane was safely built and operated. If not, they would legally tend to seek claims against the maker or the operator for damages. Insurance companies also want to know, since they are often backing claims related to having insured the flight. Regulators want to know since they are concerned about whether commercial plane makers and operators are doing what is safe and abiding by regulations. Plus, they might discover that the regulations are lax and need to be tightened or otherwise expanded.

Do those reasons also apply to the use of EDR's in cars? Some would say yes, those reasons do apply. Though a car crash might only involve one person or just a few people, while an airplane crash might involve hundreds, it is considered likewise important to know what led to the crash. Car insurers certainly want to know. Those harmed in a car crash want to know. There have been many cases of car crashes that involved one or more cars that had an EDR, and the EDR became essential for the facts of the case. Suppose a driver claims they were legally driving at the posted speed. The EDR recording can help to either verify this claim or refute it.

If you are interested in EDR's for cars, you should take a close look at the U.S. Federal Regulations in CFR Title 49, Subtitle B, Chapter V, Part 563, often referred to as "49 CFR 563" that specifies aspects about EDR's. Here's the stated scope: "This part specifies uniform, national requirements for vehicles equipped with event data recorders (EDRs) concerning the collection, storage, and retrievability of onboard motor vehicle crash event data. It also specifies requirements for vehicle manufacturers to make tools and/or methods commercially available so that crash investigators and researchers are able to retrieve data from EDRs."

How does this apply to self-driving cars?

A self-driving car is considered a car, by federal guidelines, and so it can have an EDR. Notice that I said it can have one. Allow me to offer an instance of when it would have been very handy to have had one in a self-driving car.

You might recall that I've mentioned that the Tesla fatal car crash of 2016 is an important first-case of a car crash involving a self-driving car. The federal investigation that examined the Tesla mentioned this: "The regulation does not require that vehicles be equipped with event data recorders. Equipping a vehicle with an event data recorder is completely voluntary."

It then also says this: "The Tesla Model S involved in this crash did not, nor was it required by regulation, contain an event data recorder" (for further details, see the National Transportation Safety

Board (NTSB) report, dated March 7, 2017, entitled "Driver Assistance System: Specialist's Factual Report).

No one seems to have gotten upset about this aspect in the Tesla car crash case. There wasn't any public outrage. Imagine a plane crash that had no black box. I am guessing many would wonder why there wasn't a black box in that plane. Some have quietly wondered why Tesla does not have a formal EDR. As we get more self-driving cars on the road, and I am not just referring to Tesla, but also thinking about all the car makers, I believe we'll see more self-driving car crashes, and eventually it is going to become a publicly debated issue, along with pressure on regulators to consider making it mandatory specifically for self-driving cars.

I am singling out self-driving cars over normal human-driven cars. I do this because there is ongoing debate about violating the privacy of human drivers. Some say that having an EDR on a car is a potential violation of your right to privacy. Usually, whatever is recorded by the EDR can only be reviewed under certain circumstances, and indeed about a dozen states say when it can be inspected, such as only with a court order or other special circumstances. Though there might be legal protections, there is also the possibility of hacking into the EDR. People are worried that their private related driving data might be hacked.

Others say that they don't get why anyone would believe that their driving data is such a big secret. So what that you drove for 50 miles at 40 miles per hours, and made two left turns during that driving journey? Who cares? The counter-argument is that it can reveal where you drove, if it is capturing GPS data. Maybe you don't want others to know that you drove to the shady part of town. Why should that be anyone's business other than your own? This debate continues to go on and on.

For self-driving cars, the question arises as to whether the self-driving car has any kind of expected right to privacy. You might say that the AI of the car deserves rights to privacy, but that is kind of a kilter since the AI is not alive (at least not yet, and not for a very long time, if ever, some would say).

You could say that the occupants of the self-driving car are by extension where the privacy issue will arise. It's not the self-driving car AI that needs the privacy, but the occupants that do. Those though that are worried about the emergence and safety of self-driving cars would argue that the value of the EDR data for the good of the public and the good of the innovation of self-driving cars should outweigh the privacy concerns of those occupants in the self-driving car.

They also point to today's cabs and ride sharing services. When you take a taxi today, do you have a right to privacy if that taxi happens to have an EDR in it? Most would say you do not. But then again, a taxi and owning your own self-driving car could be construed as vastly different situations.

Anyway, let's get back to the instance of the Tesla crash.

The Tesla did has its own proprietary Electronic Control Unit (ECU) that did record some data. Note thought that as stated in the NTSB report, since the regulation does not require having an EDR, and since the ECU is not an EDR, there is not any need for the ECU to have recorded data in accordance with the provisions of a federally regulated EDR: "...the data recorded by the ECU was not recorded in accordance with the regulation," which is OK since the ECU wasn't an EDR.

What does this mean? It means that the ECU did not have to record the type of data required by federal regulations for EDR's. Nor did it have to comply with the formatting requirements. It was entirely up to the car maker to decide what they thought would be valuable to record and how to record it. According to federal regulations, they are perfectly fine to do so. The regulations don't force them to do otherwise. But, some ask, should we allow such latitude? Would it be better to force the self-driving car makers to abide by the regulations?

Besides wanting to ensure that the type of data that the feds think is important for a crash investigations to then get recorded, it also allows for the feds to directly inspect the data, if the EDR regulation is used.

In the Tesla case, the ECU data was recorded in a proprietary format devised by Tesla. Here's what the federal investigation said: "...there is no commercially available tool for data retrieval and review of the ECU data. NTSD investigators had to rely on Tesla to provide the data in engineering units using proprietary manufacturer software."

Thus, the NTSB was unable to directly inspect the ECU data, which was not in the federal standard format, and nor recorded all the same types of data required by the federal government, but for which was perfectly fine for Tesla to have done.

Why does this make a difference?

Looking at another part of the NTSB investigation, here's something of interest: "The recorder data that NTSB investigators received from Tesla does not provide information about the activation of the Speed Assist system. NTSB investigators cannot determine whether the system (1) was available (i.e., no turned off), or, (2) activated during the trip on which the crash occurred."

As you can see, the NTSB had to rely on whatever Tesla was able to tell the NTSB what was there or not there. I am not implying anything was afoot. I am just saying that likely it would be generally preferred by any car crash that involves any car maker, whether it be Tesla, Ford, Toyota, or anyone, for the NTSB itself to be able to inspect the recorded data. I am betting that the public would likely want to see this occur.

Allow me to though also poke holes at the existing federal regulations. The 49 CFR 563 is woefully inadequate for self-driving cars, in my humble opinion. It requires that only 15 key variables be tracked, such as speed, airbag deployment, brakes application, etc. These are certainly essential, but insufficient. There are 30 additional variables that are encouraged to be collected, including GPS, but it is not mandatory.

Even these additional variables though are not advanced enough for self-driving cars. In other words, the advent of self-driving cars should get us to augment and revise the requirements to accommodate more kinds of data and the nature of the data to be kept.

Worse still, the EDR data only needs to have twenty seconds of data involving the crash, according to the federal regulations. This is very insufficient. In the olden days, having electronic memory in a black box was not easy to do, because it was costly to have hardened memory that could withstand the harshness of a crash, and so the time limit was allowed to be very low. Plus, the amount of space required for memory used to mean that the black box would need to be larger and heavier. This is no longer the case.

As you can see, I am a strong advocate for requiring EDR's on self-driving cars, and forcing the self-driving car makers to abide by the federal regulations, along with wanting to get the regulators to increase and modernize the federal regulations on this. I am certainly torn somewhat because I am leery of overly regulating an industry, and especially one that is going through rapid innovation. But, it seems to me, asking for a more robust black box is not overly burdening the self-driving car makers. It actually would in-the-end probably be better for self-driving car makers. When some self-driving car goes bad, it would help to point at that particular car maker, which otherwise it might be that we'll assume that all self-driving cars and car makers are bad.

Plus, it might actually protect the reputation of a self-driving car, in the sense that suppose a human driver collides with a self-driving car and claims that the self-driving car made the wrong decision. We might not know from the accident scene what really happened, and by having the EDR we might be able to piece things together, and suppose it wasn't the fault of the self-driving car then we'd have proof.

Which is going to be stronger proof, a human driver of a conventional car or a self-driving car? If we don't have any proof of what the self-driving car was doing, people will probably side with the human driver. On the other hand, if we have the word of the human driver versus the cold, hard facts of the EDR, we'd probably no longer think of it as a "he said, she said" situation, and presume that the EDR was the right indicator of what occurred.

I want to add some caution here though, which as a technologist and AI developer, I can say that we should not blindly believe whatever the EDR says. Suppose the EDR was not properly recording? There could be some flaw in the EDR software. The sensors of the self-driving car might be falsely reporting data. And so on. It could also be something intentionally done by whomever programmed the EDR to do the recording in that maybe they purposely wrote it to omit something or transform something.

All I am saying is that simply having an EDR is alone not the end-all, and for any circumstance we would need to also ensure that we can believe what the EDR claims to have recorded. Think of the movie "Minority Report" and you'll get my drift on this.

For those of you that are on your toes about self-driving cars, I am sure you might be thinking that the era of the EDR or black box is now over, since we can do over-the-air communications with a self-driving car. Those of you that are new to self-driving cars might not realize that many of the self-driving cars are sending data via usually the Internet or something comparable to the servers of the car maker (or other). Thus, there is data inside the self-driving car, and also data that is sent from the self-driving car to an external remote server. This is often done continuously during a driving journey.

We presumably don't need to dig in the rubble of a car crash and can instead go to those that control the servers and ask them to give us the data about what was going on inside the self-driving car. Not so fast!

As per the NTSB report of the Tesla crash, they summed up the concern about this reliance as follows: "In general, data stored on-board the vehicle will contain information additional to that contained on Tesla severs. Specifically, any data stored since the last auto-load event will exist only on the vehicle itself..."

In essence, the servers by any car maker are likely to not have all of the same data as was recorded by the EDR. It could be that there wasn't an over-the-air connection to allow the EDR to push its data over to the servers. It could be that the server refresh only occurs every say hour, or maybe only when triggered in certain situations. It could be that of the say 15 types of data that the EDR only pushes over 10 of the required types of data. There are a thousand reasons that whatever is on the server might not reflect the data that was recorded by the EDR.

This, though, brings up another reason to consider updating the federal regulations, since we presumably should have some means of identifying what such recording servers should or should not contain, which right now is without regulatory guidance (again, I am not saying we should burden the car makers, just offering that at least let's consider what makes reasonable sense).

If you are an AI developer like me, I would want to have as much data recorded by both the EDR and pushed over to the server as I could, which would then allow me to more thoroughly be able to discover what happened in a self-driving car crash. If the EDR gets destroyed by the car crash, it would be great to have as much as possible on the server to take a look at. Even if the EDR survives, but if it has more timely data or more extensive data, I'd want to look at both the EDR and the server. Also, suppose the EDR data gets partially corrupted, I could compare to what's on the server. Or, suppose the data when sent to the server gets corrupted, I could verify what's on the server to what the EDR says.

Of course, not everyone shares that same desire for having as much data as possible. We've already discussed here that there are privacy concerns. In addition, some wonder whether having all this data is good or bad for self-driving cars. Maybe having too much data is bad. Maybe it will become a witch hunt whenever there is a self-driving car crash. Those that want to stop the advent of self-driving cars might try to use the EDR and server data in untoward ways. Do lawyers want this data to exist or not? Do insurers want it to exist or not?

Big questions. At least we should be discussing it. Right now, nobody is paying any attention to the topic of EDR's for self-driving cars. It barely registers as even a topic for human driven cars. I hope that I have sparked some interest in the topic overall, and especially for self-driving cars.

Like it or not, I am betting we'll all eventually be discussing this topic once self-driving cars are readily available, and we are seeing regrettably self-driving car related crashes and incidents, for whatever reasons, and then people will ask, hey, what about those black boxes.

CHAPTER 16
LOOKING BEHIND YOU
FOR SELF-DRIVING CARS

CHAPTER 16

LOOKING BEHIND YOU
FOR SELF-DRIVING CARS

In college, my roommate was a car buff. He loved cars. Whenever he had the time, he would tinker with some aspect of his beloved car. At first, I thought he knew everything thing there was to know about cars. He did though have some quirks, one of which I discovered during a first-time ride with him in his pampered car. I had noticed while sitting in the passenger seat that he rarely seemed to look at his rear-view mirror. Upon closer inspection, I realized that there wasn't a mirror in his rear-view mirror.

I asked him why he did not have a mirror in his rear-view mirror. This seemed to me like a "glaring" omission that should be rectified right away. In other words, the rear-view mirror structure was mounted in the normal spot on the front windshield, but there wasn't a glass mirror inside the rear-view mirror. It was mirrorless. He then explained to me that this was done on purpose. What, I asked incredulously, could be the purpose for having a rear-view mirror that is mirrorless?

His answer: There's no reason for him to look behind himself.

Huh? This seemed to be an answer that itself was also a mystery. Why would he not need to look behind his car? He said that it was because anyone that was behind his car had the responsibility to not get in his way, and he didn't therefore envision any bona fide reason to need to look behind himself.

Note that he "cleverly" and purposely had not removed the rear-view mirror mount itself due to it legally being required by the Department of Motor Vehicles (DMV) that he had to have one. He didn't want to get a ticket from a cop and so he figured no one would ever know that he didn't have the actual mirror in the rear-view mirror. Thus, he had a rear-view mirror that he never needed to glance at and it was there solely for ornamental purposes to avoid getting fined. I pointed out that I was pretty sure that if a cop realized there wasn't a mirror he would still get a ticket, in spite of having the mount. He said that the odds of a cop realizing that there wasn't a mirror was slim, and if a cop did realize it, the issued ticket would only be a fix-it ticket that would be easy to rectify. Seemed amazing to me that he had put so much effort into this, when he could have just left the darned mirror in the thing.

This kind of boggles the mind and is pretty wild. A driver that does not believe he or she needs to look behind themselves. No need to see the traffic behind them. Just drive forward and anything behind you will need to take care of itself. Life is apparently forward looking, not backward looking.

Where else do we see this kind of logic? In some of today's self-driving cars.

That's right, some of today's self-driving cars do not seem to be worried about looking behind the car. At the Cybernetics Self-Driving Car Institute, we are expanding the capabilities of self-driving cars to appropriately utilize awareness of what is behind the car.

You might be saying to yourself that most cars already now have a back-up cam, and indeed it is gradually becoming a mandated feature on American cars, thus they can "see" behind themselves. A back-up cam though is just used for backing up, when you are moving relatively slowly, and in reverse. It is not used when you are moving forward. Tesla's have a radar unit on the front grill of the car, but no radar at the back of the car. They have cameras pointing at the back on the Model 3, but no other sensory devices for this purpose.

Why would you care about what's behind your car?

Well, imagine that you are sitting at an intersection due to a red light and a car coming up behind you is coming at you very quickly. Your judgement tells you that the wayward car is going to ram into the rear of your car. You quickly move out of the way to avoid getting crashed into. This happened to me a few months ago. I did a risky safety maneuver by going into the intersection (luckily it was open) to avoid the careless car that was coming upon me – presumably the driver and had not realized that the light was red. Had I not moved out of the way, it would have been smash city. If I hadn't been looking at my rear-view mirror, I would not have known to move out of the way.

For most starting drivers such as teenagers, they are instructed to always be checking their rear-view mirror. Glance at it frequently. Know what cars are behind you. Know how fast they are moving. Know if they are directly behind you, or whether they are in a different lane. Be aware of your surroundings. Be watching for motorcyclists that are coming up behind you. Indeed, during my morning commute on the freeway, I often see cars ahead of me that have realized a motorcycle is coming up upon them, and it is weaving throughout traffic as it cuts on the lane lines. Those observant drivers that are watching their rear-view mirror move over slightly from the lane line to give the motorcyclist a little added space to pass. It is a courtesy and also a means to reduce the chances that the motorcyclist will hit their car.

Most of the motorcyclist accidents that I witness on the freeway are typically due to a car driver that did not realize the motorcycle was coming up behind them. Whether the human driver was lazy or just being forgetful, they made a lane change and plowed right into a motorcyclist. Believe it or not, this happens about once per week during my five days a week freeway commute. Over and over again, I see a car make a lane change and a motorcyclist that gets caught going forward and ramming into the lane switching car. Did the driver of the car look in their rear-view mirror to see what was behind them? Probably not.

We expect teenage drivers to be using their rear-view mirrors whenever they make a lane change. The recommended practice by the

DMV involves first checking your rear-view mirror, and then looking over your shoulder as a double-check that its clear to make the lane change, along with using your side-view mirrors. Suppose we told a teenage driver they did not need to look in their rear-view mirror, they did not need to look at their side-view mirrors, and they did not need to look over their shoulder. I believe you would likely agree we'd have chaos and accidents aplenty.

This is what we're going to also experience with many self-driving cars, until the self-driving car makers get more in-tune with considering what goes on behind a car. Self-driving cars equipped with LIDAR are fortunately able to "see" behind the car. By using laser pulses, the LIDAR can potentially identify objects behind the car. I say the word potentially because this assumes that the LIDAR is being used for a 360-degree perspective around the car. Some LIDAR have a narrower Field of Vision (FOV) and do not encompass a full 360-degree viewpoint. Even the ones that do have a 360-degree FOV are often programmed to not be especially mindful of what is behind the car.

Let me explain this a bit further in terms of what is technically going on (see too my article about sensor fusion for self-driving cars). The LIDAR that is able to collect a 360-degree view is simply gathering data. It is up to whatever AI component is doing sensor fusion to figure out what the data actually means. If the AI system is programmed to not utilize the data from the LIDAR that shows what is happening behind the car, it makes little difference that the LIDAR is collecting it at all. This is equivalent to having a teenage driver that looks in their rear-view mirror, sees what is going on behind their car, but is unable to mentally process this visualization and just proceeds to drive as though they really hadn't looked at the rear-view mirror at all.

Why wouldn't an AI system make sure to squeeze every ounce of data from the LIDAR? It could be that the developers didn't realize that using rearward data would be important. They might have thought the same thing that my college roommate believed, namely that having data from behind you isn't particularly important. Or, they might have been rushed to develop the AI for the self-driving car and didn't have the time or resources to develop code to analyze rearward data. One might also consider that processing the rearward data takes processing power and so you need to have more processors on the self-driving car to do this kind of calculating. It can be a cost factor of having more processors and so therefore it increases the cost of the self-driving car. Another possibility is that the rearward data is only analyzed for the most obvious of deadly circumstances, but otherwise the data is ignored.

For example, suppose a car is coming up behind you at a fast rate of speed. Let's suppose the LIDAR is detecting this object, in this case the car coming up behind you. In the virtual model of the world surrounding the self-driving car, the AI needs to figure out that the car is coming up toward the self-driving car, and it is coming up at a fast speed. Does a fast speed mean that the other car will hit the self-driving car? No, not necessarily. It could be that the other car will change lanes, sometimes at the last moment, and avoid rear-ending into the self-driving car. Some AI programmers assume that the other car is being driven in a rationale way and that "obviously" the other driver will make sure to avoid hitting the self-driving car.

This belies the fact that every day we have thousands of rear-end accidents taking place. The rearward data should be used to make predictions about what might happen. Each day, during my morning commute, I am mentally calculating whether a car rushing up behind me will potentially ram into my car. If I think the risk factor is high enough, I take evasive action. We should expect that our self-driving cars should use the same logic (see my article about defensive driving for self-driving cars).

Self-driving cars should be collecting rearward data, they should be merging it within the virtual model of their surroundings, and they need to ascertain probabilities of potential dangers and how to drive defensively because of the dangers. Elon Musk has said that he doesn't believe that LIDAR is needed for self-driving cars.

In which case, if you believe as I do that knowing what's behind you is essential for a true self-driving car, he's betting that cameras alone are sufficient for rearward inspection. Cameras have numerous limitations and so having just one kind of sensory device for rearward data collection is dicey.

Besides detecting cars that are approaching you, it is also important to keep track of pedestrians that are behind you. When I was driving down an alley last year, and though I was moving very slowly, a pedestrian walked right up behind my car and walked right into it. I admit that I had not seen him, even though I was glancing at my rear-view mirror from time-to-time. I heard a thump on the trunk of my car, and imagine my shock to look back and see that a human was bent over on the trunk of my car. I even thought at first that it was a scam. Maybe the person wanted to claim an accident had happened and get me to pay them off or maybe file an insurance claim.

But, anyway, the point is that anything can be behind a car and be something that the driver needs to know about. An approaching car, an approaching motorcyclist, an approaching pedestrian, an approaching bicyclist, an approaching skateboarder, and so on. Emergency vehicles are another category of important objects that can be approaching from behind (see my other books about emergency vehicle detection for self-driving cars). I fervently argue that we need to have multiple types of sensors to detect what's behind a self-driving car, and we need to have the sensor fusion and AI that well uses that information.

Due to economic reasons, self-driving car makers are tending to have just one form of sensor technology for looking rearward. Each type of sensor has its own limitations. Combining the perspective of multiple sensors is key for driving safety. To me, a true self-driving car ought to have LIDAR, cameras, and radar for rearward data collection. If we want to ultimately achieve a Level 5 self-driving car (see my article about the Richter scale of self-driving cars), I suggest we will need multiple types of sensors and a more rigorous effort of AI software that can stitch together the data and take appropriate actions. Watch out for what's behind you!

CHAPTER 17
IN-CAR VOICE COMMANDS NLP FOR
SELF-DRIVING CARS

CHAPTER 17

IN-CAR VOICE COMMANDS FOR SELF-DRIVING CARS

Sometimes I yell at my car. For example, the other day I wanted to quickly accelerate to get out of a tough situation and so I put my foot to the metal and gave the car a rush of gas in hopes that it would sprint forward. The car did lurch forward, but not as fast as I imagined it should, and so I yelled at it, exhorting it to go faster. In case you are worried that I mistreat my car, there are other times that I whisper sweet nothings to it. Like the other day it had been faithful and worked without a hitch when I drove out to Phoenix from Southern California, taking it through desert temperatures that rose to an incredible 115 degrees. For its bravery and honor in doing the trip, I thanked it heartily.

I try not to anthropomorphize my car, though a lot of people do. They give their cars cute pet-like names and pamper their car. They speak to it as though it is a father confessor. Once we are all using self-driving cars, and those are packed with sophisticated AI systems, it will be interesting to see if people go even further with treating their car like a fellow human. Already, we have Alexa and Siri as natural language processing (NLP) sisters and brothers. Cars are already including on-board NLP capabilities for primarily entertainment purposes. You can tell your car to play the latest hot music tracks.

A few cars are also allowing voice commands to do some other tasks, such as telling the car to roll down a window or lock the car doors. One ongoing question about self-driving cars is whether or not the human occupants will be able to speak to the car and interact with the self-driving car. I don't really though see this as a question per se, since to me it is obvious that yes we will have self-driving cars that interact with the occupants. This is a must.

At the Cybernetic Self-Driving Car Institute, I have been closely studying the interaction between humans and what they would want a self-driving car to discuss with them, and we have been developing NLP to do so. Allow me to describe what we have discovered.

Most would concede that somehow the self-driving car will at least need to know the destination of where the occupants want to go. I suppose you could use your smart phone to convey this to the self-driving car, but I see it as a simple enough added capability that you would directly speak to the car and chat with it about your desired destination. At this juncture, those that are willing to agree that the occupant would perhaps want or need to speak to the self-driving car about the desired destination, they seem to think that after doing so that then there is no other reason to have the occupants interact with the self-driving car.

Well, suppose that I have told the self-driving car to take me to work, but I then change my mind midway of the driving journey and decide I want to head back home, maybe because I left the stove on or because I inadvertently left my garage door open. What about that? Those that think the occupant only needs to give a final destination at the start of a driving journey seem completely oblivious to the aspect that we often change our minds during a driving effort and want to go someplace else instead. Now, I realize that when you use a taxi or an Uber that you normally indicate upfront your desired destination, and you don't change it midcourse, but this is not how people use their everyday cars. Everyday driving is quite different than using a ride sharing or ride providing service.

Indeed, let's try another example of altering your course during a driving journey. You are on the freeway and heading to work, which it turns out is an hour-long commute. You decide you must have coffee to fully wake-up. So, after about 20 minutes on the freeway, you start looking for a McDonald's golden arches that is near to the freeway, and then take the next exit to swing through and get yourself some java. It wasn't part of your original plan of the trip. It came up spontaneously. This happens all the time during any kind of driving trip.

Thus, you would need to have some means to communicate with the self-driving car during a driving journey. Rather than having to use your smart phone, it makes a lot of sense and just seems easier to go ahead and speak to your car and tell it what you want to do. Suppose you assign your self-driving car the name of Lauren, you would then say to your self-driving car, "Lauren, take me to work" and then later on when you got the urge to have coffee you might say "Lauren, go to the nearest McDonald's" or something like that.

These kinds of commands to your self-driving car are relatively benign in that you are essentially interacting with a GPS, which we already do anyway. Of course, if you have a GPS in your car today, it is still you that currently is actually driving the car, and not the GPS system. As you know, the GPS has various limitations, and so sometimes you likely drive differently than what the GPS tells you to do.

The other day I was coming up to an intersection and the GPS told me to make a left turn. The left turn lane was packed with cars and it would have taken forever to make that left turn, plus it was a risky left turn since there wasn't an arrow specifically for making the left turn. I opted to instead go past the intersection, make a right turn up ahead, make another right turn to come around the block, and then was able to effectively have achieved getting onto the street that the GPS advised.

I mention this because we might not always be satisfied with how a self-driving car is driving us to a destination. Besides wanting to alter the final destination, or wanting to have midcourse changes to go to other intermediate destinations, you might also want to tell the car specific ways to go. You might say don't make the left turn and instead go around to get there. Or, you might tell the self-driving car to avoid a neighborhood that you know is dangerous and you are worried about driving through it. There are lots of aspects that would involve you wanting to interact with the self-driving car about the path it is taking.

Currently, most GPS are somewhat passive and whatever destination you request, it will indicate how to get there. It will also often offer alternative paths and let you pick one. It will provide traffic updates and try to find more optimal routes during the driving journey. All of this requires further interaction with the human occupant. This also raises another aspect, namely should the human be able to instruct the self-driving car to go places that don't make any sense to go?

If I get into my car today and I ask my GPS how I can get from Los Angeles to New York, the GPS will gladly indicate it. It is still up to me to make the actual drive. With a self-driving car, suppose you tell your car to drive from Los Angeles to New York. Should the self-driving car obediently comply and just go ahead and start to make that drive? Maybe you as the human indicator have mistakenly said New York and you meant some other closer destination. Or, maybe you said New York but have no idea how long a drive it is. Let's assume that the self-driving car didn't tell you how long a drive it is, or mentioned it but you didn't happen to see or hear what it said. The next thing you know, your car is headed on a really long journey.

Worse still, suppose I give a destination that is life threatening. I tell my self-driving car to drive off the end of the local pier. Should the self-driving car do this? These are part of the ethics aspects of self-driving cars (see my other books on ethics and self-driving cars). Presumably, our self-driving cars should have some kind of checks-and-balances so that we cannot readily command the car to kill us.

This brings up another facet of uttering commands to a self-driving car. There are driving instructions that a human might want to indicate to the self-driving car. So far, we have focused on instructions related to the destinations and geographical locations. You might have other preferences too. Specific commands would consist of telling the self-driving car to "speed-up" or to "slow down." These are though ambiguous commands. If you tell a friend to speed-up while they are driving, what does this mean? Are you saying to go just 1 mile per hour faster, or 5 miles per hour faster, or 20 miles per hour faster? The self-driving car would need to get clarification from the occupant.

But, suppose that the self-driving car is going 15 miles per hour and it is a school zone. You as the occupant say to the self-driving car to go faster. It asks you how much faster. You say 10 miles per hour faster. Let's assume that the school zone has a posted speed limit of 15 miles per hour. Should the self-driving car go faster, as you have asked, even though it will now be exceeding the allowed speed limit? Probably, it should not. The self-driving car needs to be disobedient when needed. At the same time, suppose you are in your self-driving car and bleeding from a severe wound, and you need to get to a hospital as fast as possible. Maybe in this case you would want the self-driving car to go as fast as it can, though presumably it should be nonetheless still aware of driving safely (in other words, it might be willing to exceed the posted speed limit, but do so with still having safety as a crucial part of the driving task).

One important point then is that during the dialogue between the self-driving car and the human, the self-driving car must be able and willing to talk-back to the human. In other words, the self-driving car cannot just blindly obey any commands spoken to it. This would create many very dangerous situations. The self-driving car NLP needs to interpret what the human has stated and then let the human know what qualms there are about it. The self-driving car should echo back what was said, and then offer any concerns such as whether the request is impossible, or deadly, or illegal, or whatever issues there might be.

I realize that people aren't going to like this kind of talk-back, at least at first. If you have ever interacted with Alexa or Siri, you already know how frustrating it can be to get those NLP's to even understand what seem to be simple requests and ones that aren't life-or-death in nature. We need even stronger NLP for dealing with interactions of the self-driving car and the humans. There can't be ambiguity or aspects left to chance. The self-driving car needs to know precisely what the instruction consists of, and whether or not it is in the end a sensible instruction for the self-driving car to carry out. This would be equivalent to having a taxi driver that would certainly question a passenger that wanted to drive off the end of the pier or do some other kind of untoward maneuver.

I have so far discussed relatively simplistic commands, but there are also more complex compound kinds of commands that humans would want to utter. I might say this to my self-driving car: "Lauren, take me to my favorite night club, but first stop at Eric's place to pick him up, and during the trip I want to go along the ocean and see the sunset." Parse that. I have indicated to go to a night club, specifically my favorite one (which maybe the system knows of, due to my frequently going there). If the parsing stopped there and only knew about going to the night club, the self-driving car would drive to that destination. But, I have also said we need to pick-up Eric before going to the night club. The self-driving car now has an intermediate destination, and presumably knows somehow what Eric's address is. To make things more complicated, I have indicated that I want to have the path include going near the ocean, and so the self-driving car needs to figure out what path that would be.

A taxi driver would presumably easily be able to parse such a compound sentence. For NLP to do this, it's tricky. The self-driving car will need to echo back to the human what it believes has been stated, doing so in a reworded fashion to ensure that clarification is achieved. It would need to get confirmation from the human. And, probably even double-check the confirmation and not just allow a muttered "yes" by the human to be sufficient to engage. This kind of man-machine voice interaction is very sophisticated and today's NLP can barely do something like this. Furthermore, it needs to be done in a manner that isn't overly irritating to the human. Imagine a taxi driver that doesn't understand your language and that's basically how today's NLP is.

Who is uttering these commands to the self-driving car? I keep saying the human does, but who is the human? You might say to me that it is obviously whomever is the occupant of the car. The human occupant should presumably be the human telling the self-driving car what to do and where to go. If there is only one person in the car, maybe this a reasonable notion. That assumes that the human occupant in the self-driving car is authorized to actually make use of the self-driving car and is capable of doing so.

When my son was about 6 years old, he delighted in sitting in the car and pretend that he was driving the car. Even if he had the key to the car, he was too small and unable to comprehend how to actually drive the car. Suppose that in the future, your 6 year old jumps into your self-driving car and tells it to drive him to his friend's house. Is this a valid command to the self-driving car? You might say that of course it is not valid, the occupant is too young. But, the occupant doesn't presumably need to be able to drive the car (if this is a true self-driving car of a Level 5), and so why not allow the boy to command the car? Indeed, there are going to be parents that like the idea of not having to drive around their children and just let the self-driving car do so.

I have already predicted that we're going to have some sizable debates about who can command a self-driving car and what policies and laws there will be. Do we really want children to be in self-driving cars all by themselves? What if the self-driving car breaks down in the middle of nowhere? What if the child gets confused and gives commands to the self-driving car that endanger themselves? These are all thorny public policy questions and will likely end-up becoming various laws.

Suppose that there is more than one occupant in a self-driving car. Now, how does the self-driving car deal with human provided commands? Two adults are in the self-driving car. They are arguing about where to go. One says to the self-driving car, go to the park. The other one says go to the mall. You can almost see the self-driving car going in one direction, then making a U-turn to go in the other direction, and otherwise being whipped back-and-forth and just blindly obeying whatever is stated.

Currently, this is settled by the fact that there is just one driver of the car. There might be many so-called "backseat drivers" but they are not able to do anything other than provide commentary. It is today the human actually at the driving controls that decides what happens. We will now have an AI system at the driving controls. How will it deal with the problem of having multiple occupants and potentially multiple commands, and conflicting commands?

One approach involves having a "designated driver" that means just one person in the self-driving car is able to command the self-driving car. A father and his two children are in a self-driving car. The father is the "designated driver" and commands the self-driving car. The children are not listened to by the self-driving car. This of course means that the self-driving car has to somehow learn the voice of the father so as to do voice recognition and realize that it is the father speaking. This could also be a security measure that only the father's voice can activate and command the self-driving car.

This seems like a viable solution. Except, suppose the father suddenly faints in the self-driving car due to fatigue. The self-driving car is now operating without any human "designated driver" and it has been instructed to ignore any other voices other than the voice of the father. This is not a good situation. We either concede to this risk, or we allow that other voices can be allowed to provide commands, perhaps as "secondary drivers," though we put restrictions on when and in what way those other voices can give commands that will be obeyed by the self-driving car.

One approach that some self-driving car makers are considering involves having a remote human operator that can interact with the occupants and the self-driving car (see my other books on remote piloting of self-driving cars). Similar to an On-Star kind of system, there would be a remote human operator that could talk with the occupants, and then based on human judgement decide how to instruct the self-driving car. People are probably going to accept this approach for ride sharing and taxis, but it is doubtful they will find this as satisfactory for their own self-driving car that they have purchased.

Overall, my key point in this discussion has been that we will absolutely want our self-driving cars to interact with the occupants. Those self-driving car makers and engineers that keep saying that this is either unnecessary or not viable are short-sighted in their vision of self-driving cars. They tend to think that humans are stupid and should just act like sheep and get into their self-driving cars, and do nothing other than say where they want to go. Having a car offers a great deal of freedom, and people want to exercise that freedom, whether it is in a regular car or a self-driving car.

Advances in NLP will help to engage human occupants in a dialogue about the self-driving car and where it is going, how it will drive, etc. This dialogue will occur not just at the start of a driving trip, but throughout a driving trip. It will involve simple commands and complex compound commands. It will require the self-driving car to interpret the commands, determine who can provide a command, echo commands back, affirm a command, and carry out a command, assuming that the command is possible, legal, etc. This for some developers is considered an edge problem of self-driving cars. We see it as a core problem because ultimately people are going to decide whether to use or not use a self-driving car based on not only what it can do but how it interacts with them

CHAPTER 18

WHEN SELF-DRIVING CARS GET PULLED OVER BY A COP

CHAPTER 18

WHEN SELF-DRIVING CARS
GET PULLED OVER BY A COP

Years ago, I was driving up to Silicon Valley from Southern California, cruising along at top speed on the freeway, and ended-up getting a speeding ticket in a somewhat unusual manner. Here's what happened.

I was driving along and minding my own business. Other cars were zooming past me, going much faster than the posted speed limit. Mile by mile, I gradually let my speed climb. I still wasn't going as fast as those other cars, but admittedly was now going faster than the speed limit. I knew of course that there was some risk in getting a speeding ticket. But, it was a clear sunny day, I could see a great distance behind me and in front of me, and figured that I would certainly spot a police car and then could reduce my speed before they would realize that I was speeding. There were posted signs on the freeway that said they used planes to spot speeders, so I was even keeping my eyes aimed upward in anticipation of spotting any low flying planes in the empty blue sky.

After a few hours of driving above the speed limit, my being on-watch had waned. Guess I am not much of a criminal in that sense. Suddenly, I noticed back in the distance a highway patrol car behind me and it was coming up very fast. Yikes! I was tempted to pump my brakes, but then I realized it might suggest to the patrol officer that I was trying to reduce speed and therefore must be speeding. So, instead, I just let up on the accelerator and prayed as I watched my speed inch its way down to the allowed speed limit.

Maybe he was too far away to know I was speeding. Maybe he would be more interested in the other cars that had been passing me, since they were going much faster than me. They were the true law breakers! Well, he came up to me, got into the lane to my left, drew in alignment with my car. I assumed at this point that he wasn't going to pull me over and I had gotten lucky about the whole situation. Surprisingly, he looked over at me, and then made a motion with his two hands of the kind that you would use when scolding a child. He then accelerated rapidly and rushed up ahead.

I decided that a scolding was fine and better than having gotten an actual traffic ticket. My nerves settled down and I opted to remain driving at the speed limit. About five miles later, I could see ahead to the right of the road that there were several cars stopped and parked. This seemed odd. This was a stretch of road that had nothing on it. No reason to be stopped. From time to time, I'd see a car stopped with its hood up, apparently suffering from engine troubles. But I had never seen a slew of cars parked on this open stretch of highway.

As I neared the line of cars that were parked on the shoulder of the roadway, I slowed down due to being concerned that maybe something was amiss up ahead. Road out? Bridge down? Eight-hundred-pound gorilla in the roadway? I then noticed that at the front of the line of parked cars was the highway patrol car that had gone past me earlier. Furthermore, the police officer was standing outside next to his patrol car. He was waving at me and motioning for me to pull over.

I pulled over and got behind the other parked cars on the shoulder. Whatever was going on, it seemed serious. It was also dangerous because being parked on the shoulder of a highway that had big trucks and cars traveling at high speeds is not a safe place to be. Anyway, I waited to see what was going to happen next.

The officer came up to my car. I rolled down my window. He had those tough guy sunglasses on and looked like someone not to mess with. He then proceeded to tell me that he was pulling me over for speeding. Me, and about a dozen of my fellow criminals. He had gone to the head of the pack of cars, pulled that first car over, and then one by one pulled the rest of us over. At first, I was dumbfounded and had never realized that such a procedure existed. I wondered too how he had known of my speeding. Turns out he claimed that their police plane had been hovering over the highway and spotted all of us speeding.

To this day, some of my friends say that I should have ignored his motioning for me to pull over. My friends claim that I should have just kept driving and that he would have been unlikely to come after me, given that he had about a dozen other scofflaws already in-hand. I could have maybe claimed that I didn't see his motioning or misunderstood his motioning. On the other hand, I tell my friends that turning a speeding ticket into an all-out police pursuit would probably not have been a wise move.

Why do I tell this story? I tell it because one aspect of self-driving cars that we need to consider involves having a self-driving car pull over when a police request is made to do so. This is what we at the Cybernetics Self-Driving Car Institute call an "edge problem" of self-driving cars (see my other books on Edge Problems for self-driving cars). This is something that does not happen very often, but it can happen, and when it does happen then the self-driving car should be able to respond.

Some of you will argue that there should never be a cause for a self-driving car to be pulled over by the police. In this view, a self-driving car is always going to be a legal driver. I have debunked this in prior books of mine. Self-driving cars are going to potentially do actions that can be construed as an illegal act and so legitimately be pulled over. Even if the self-driving car is being driven legally, suppose the front license plate is missing from the car and it's a state that requires a front license plate. You can get pulled over for that. Or, suppose that the self-driving car has been used in the committing of a crime, like say it was used by a bank robber. The police might want to pull over the self-driving car, even though the self-driving car itself has not done anything wrong.

I hope this convinces you that it is possible that a police officer would want to pull over a self-driving car. Do not cling to the naïve view that this won't ever happen.

The next aspect is then what is to be done when a police officer does want to pull over a self-driving car. How will they signal to the self-driving car, and how will the self-driving car know what the signal means?

Those of you living in the future would say that the advent of V2V (Vehicle-to-Vehicle) communication will allow for a police car to send an electronic communication to the self-driving car and tell it to pull over. Though this is certainly possible and a likely future, we are many years away from that future. It will be a long time before today's cars are outfitted with V2V. I wouldn't hold my breath about the idea of assuming that self-driving cars will be using V2V with police cars anytime soon.

Another response to the being-pulled-over aspect is that it would be the responsibility of the human driver in the self-driving car to do so. In other words, the human driver in the car should be watching for a police officer that wants them to pull over, and then the human should take over the controls from the self-driving car to enact the pull-over. This is kind of sufficient for the level of self-driving cars of 0 to 3, but not what I believe should happen for level 4, and definitely is not what is intended to happen at level 5 (see my other books on the Richter scale for self-driving cars).

In short, we do need to have some means for a self-driving car to do this:

a) Detect that a police instruction to pull-over is taking place
b) Signal to the police that the self-driving car is going to comply
c) Find a means to safely pull-over and come to a stop
d) Adjust the stopping and location as instructed by police
e) Alert or inform the occupants of the SD car of the situation
f) Come to a safe stop and turn-off the engine as warranted

Let's take a close look at these aspects.

Detection that a police officer is possibly wanting you to pull over will usually occur by a police vehicle that has its flashing lights going and possibly is blaring its siren. They will normally come up behind your vehicle, directly behind it, and this is an indication they want you to pull over. Note that this is different than when a police car is traveling on alert as an emergency vehicle. In that case, the police car is going past you, while in this case they are coming up directly to you. This can be a somewhat tricky detection because they might come up behind you and really want to get around you, but have not yet found an opening to do so. In any case, it's a pretty solid sign that they want you to pull over.

Using the rear camera and radar, along with LIDAR, you can detect the police car and its flashing lights by the images and the speed and location of the vehicle. Though very few self-driving cars are currently audio equipped to listen for sound, we have added this sensory capability to our self-driving cars. The sound of the siren is another clue to the approaching police car that wants to pull you over.

Indeed, often a police car will get behind you and then give a verbal command to pull over, doing so via their loud speaker. Self-driving cars that don't have any listening devices won't know this is taking place. The comprehension of what is being said is a hard problem to solve, even though there are solutions such as Alexa and Siri as voice language processing, but in this case it is outdoors, it is mumbled, it is via a loudspeaker, noisy, and so discerning intelligible speech is hard. On the other hand, nearly anything spoken can be considered another likely clue of being pulled over.

This brings up another aspect about self-driving cars. Many self-driving car makers are assuming that the occupants of the car are not interacting with the self-driving car. Our viewpoint is that it is essential that occupants can communicate with the self-driving car. In this case, as a case in point, the occupants could tell the self-driving car that there is a police officer wanting the self-driving car to pull over. The self-driving car can either take their word for it and abide, or it might already have detected other clues such as the police car following them and thus combine the two indications together to confirm that indeed the self-driving car needs to pull over.

Some would say that if the occupants can communicate with the self-driving car that then there is no need at all for the self-driving car to have to ferret out whether a police car wants them the self-driving car to pull over. Presumably, the occupants can just tell the self-driving car when it should pull over. We don't agree with this generalized aspect.

Keep in mind that there are circumstances wherein the occupant might be unaware of the police request, such as if the occupant has gone unconscious. This does though bring up a thorny issue. Suppose the occupants of the self-driving car do not want to be pulled over by the police. This is the scenario of the bank robbers that are in the self-driving car. Keeping in mind that it is generally lawful for a police officer to pull over a car, it really in some ways can be argued that it doesn't matter whether the occupants want to be pulled over or not. I certainly didn't want to pull over when I had the highway patrolman motion me, but I was obligated to do so.

Once the self-driving car has arrived at the notion that it needs to pull over, we then enter into the next stage of this process. If possible, the self-driving car should signal to the police officer that it is going to comply. This is important because otherwise the police officer might become concerned that the self-driving car is trying to make a getaway. A human driver would usually turn on their turn indicator to signal that yes, they are going to get over. Using the conspicuity features of a self-driving car, the self-driving car should signal to the police officer that it is going to pull over.

Next, the self-driving car has to find a suitable spot to pull over. This in one sense should be something that the self-driving car is already considering, even prior to the police coming up. I say this because we believe that a self-driving car should always be calculating where it would be safe to stop. In other words, while driving, it is always possible that a car might need to pull over. Human drivers aren't usually continually considering this notion, but to some degree their subconscious is kind of aware of their surroundings and generally knows when things look safe or not. We always have this being run in the background by the self-driving car AI.

A self-driving car should not do reckless acts like coming to a stop in the middle of an intersection in response to the police indication to pull over. Alleys are usually bad, as would be any terrain that is rough and not suitable for driving onto. Preferably, the area to stop should be well lit and safe to be parked in, like a wide shoulder or perhaps even exiting a road to get into a parking lot. Once the car has found such a spot, sometimes a police officer gives further direction, such as ordering a driver to drive ahead fifteen feet, or pull into a driveway. The self-driving car tries to interpret such commands, though as mentioned earlier this is currently a hard problem.

During the time that the self-driving car is pulling over, one added aspect would be to potentially call 911 and report that the self-driving car is pulling over at the request of a police officer. The 911 would then relay to the police car that the self-driving car is trying to comply. Human drivers can do the same thing, though it is somewhat rarely done. In rare cases too, the officer tells 911 to tell the driver to take action. This is somewhat a better approach to receiving verbal commands since the amount of noise on the phone line is likely much less than what is commanded via a loudspeaker.

After safely settling into whatever spot has been found to stop the car, the engine would normally be turned-off by a human driver. In the case of a self-driving car, the question arises as to whether or not it makes sense to turn off the engine. If the use of the engine is required to generate power for the self-driving car, then turning off the engine will put the self-driving car AI out of commission. If the AI is powered separately then it is possible to go ahead and turn off the engine of the car.

The rolling down of the window to allow for the officer to talk with the occupants could be an automatic feature, or it could left to the occupants to manually do (or verbally command the self-driving car to do). Providing of a car registration will be for now still likely a paper-based exercise, though in the future it is info that can be readily available electronically and transmitted to the officer in that manner.

Trying to talk you way out of a ticket is not something that we envision a self-driving car to do, but, hey, maybe that's a future feature that consumers will want. In any case, seriously, the ability of a self-driving car to pull over when instructed by a police officer is a useful and usable aspect for a self-driving car to know how to do.

We covered here the aspects of a police vehicle that comes up from behind to signal to pull over, but as my story indicated earlier there are other ways this can happen too. Also, another aspect about self-driving cars will be all of the data they are collecting while driving, and whether or not this info should be given to the police. If a police officer claims your self-driving car was speeding, and you refute the claim, you might want to dig into the data being collected by the self-driving car as support for your claim that you weren't speeding. This also then raises issues about the security of the data and whether you could have doctored it for purposes of supporting your claim.

CHAPTER 19

BRAINJACKING NEUROPROSTHETUS FOR SELF-DRIVING CARS

CHAPTER 19

BRAINJACKING PROSTHETUS
FOR SELF-DRIVING CARS

Be ready to have you mind hijacked by what I am about to tell you.

Let's not get ahead of ourselves, though, and so we should start the story at the beginning.

For the future of self-driving cars, we want to ultimately have "true" self-driving cars. By this use of the word "true," I am referring to the notion that a true self-driving car is one that can entirely drive the car by itself, and does not need any human intervention during the driving task. This is considered a Level 5 self-driving car (see my other books on the Richter scale for self-driving cars).

The AI of the car is able to deal with any driving situation, and be able to respond in the same manner that a human driver could respond. There is no need to have a human driver in the self-driving car, and instead all of the humans in the self-driving car are merely considered as occupants or passengers. Even if there is a human driver that so happens to be in the self-driving car, their ability to drive is unrelated to the driving of that self-driving car.

The levels 1 through 4 of a self-driving car require that a human driver be ready to intervene in the driving task. The human driver must be present in the car whenever the self-driving component is active and driving the car. The human driver must be ready to take over control of the car, doing so perhaps even at a moment's notice (see my other books on the human factors for self-driving cars). The human driver cannot allow themselves to become overly distracted and distant from the driving task. If the human driver does become severely distracted, they endanger the safety of themselves, and endanger the safety of the other occupants, and they endanger the safety of anyone around the self-driving car, such as other cars and their drivers, pedestrians, and the like.

What do I mean by saying that a human driver might become severely distracted? I suppose I am using too strong a word. If the self-driving car is going on the highway at 80 miles per hour, and if the human driver that is supposed to be ready to take over the controls is watching a video or reading the newspaper, it is chancy that they will be able to properly and rapidly take over control of the car, if needed to do so. They would need to first become aware that there is a need to take over control of the self-driving car. This might happen by the self-driving car alerting them, such as flashing a light at the human driver or making a chime or tone.

But, the human driver cannot assume that the self-driving car will be wise enough to warn them about taking over control. It could be that the self-driving car is getting itself into a dire situation and the AI does not even realize it. Therefore, the human driver should be paying enough attention to know that they might need to take over control of the car. This can also occur if the AI itself or some part of the self-driving car automation is failing. If a key sensor fails, the self-driving car might not be a viable driver any longer. Whether it warns the human driver or not, if the human driver suspects that the automation is faltering, they are expected to take over control of the car.

The Level 5 self-driving car is instead completely different. It assumes that no human driver is needed, ever. For this assumption, I have referred to a Level 5 car as a moonshot. To be able to develop automation that can fully drive a car, in all situations, and act as a human being acts, showcasing human intelligence that is required to fully drive a car, I assure you this is a huge stretch goal. Indeed, Apple CEO Tim Cook have rightfully referred to this as the mother of all AI projects. The cognitive capabilities needed to handle a car, in all situations, and not rely upon a human, this is something of an incredible feat and one that if we can pull off means that AI will be able to do lots of other nifty things.

The gap between a Level 4 self-driving car and a Level 5 self-driving car is considered by some to be minor. I consider the gap to be enormous. It is a gap the size of the Grand Canyon. Getting us from the dependence on a human driver of Level 4, and over into the realm of no human driver of a Level 5, this is a leap of belief and faith that we will get there. Those last "few" aspects that we need to do to get away from relying upon a human driver are not just leftovers. They are the final mile that will take a tremendous amount of effort and breakthroughs to reach.

Can we make that jump from Level 4 to Level 5? Maybe. Maybe not. No one really knows. I realize that there are daily predictions of when we will see a Level 5 self-driving car, but you need to carefully review what those claims are about.

Most of the pundits making those predictions don't seem to have laid out, item by item, all the cognitive aspects that would need to be done to fully drive a car with automation. They also don't seem to have carefully reviewed the sensory capabilities of cars and connected the dots that it is both a mind and body question. The "mind" part of the AI for the self-driving car needs incredible capabilities, and it also needs the sensory "body" aspects to be able to likewise perform the driving task.

Again, I want to emphasize that a Level 5 self-driving car needs to be able to be driven entirely by the automation, and be driven wherever a human driver can drive. This means that the Level 5 self-driving car can't be limited to driving only on the highways. It must be able to drive on the highways, on city streets, in the suburbs, and so on. Any situation you can think of, that's where the Level 5 must have proficiency to drive. And, the driving obviously has to be safe. In other words, if you hand me the keys to a Level 5 (alleged) self-driving car, and it turns out that upon using it, the self-driving car crashes because it couldn't figure out how to navigate a mountain road that a human driver could drive, that's not a Level 5 self-driving car.

Let's be clear, you cannot announce that a self-driving car is a Level 5 simply because you wish it so. It needs to walk the talk, so to speak.

Now, suppose that we try and try, but we just cannot develop AI sufficiently to reach a Level 5. Maybe it's an impossible goal. Or, maybe it is possible, but it will be centuries before we perfect AI sufficiently to be able to do so.

Should we then just settle on Level 4 self-driving cars? Would we say to ourselves, hey, we don't know when or if ever we can get to Level 5, but at least we got to Level 4?

We could say that. Or, we could try to find another way to get us to Level 5.

Okay, here's where we jump the shark, so to speak, and think outside the box. Are you ready to think outside the box?

Suppose we augment the AI of the self-driving car with the incredible powers of the human mind, making a connection between the AI of the self-driving car and a human driver in the car. Wait, you say, isn't this the same thing as needing a human driver in the Level 4 and below levels?

Not exactly. Here's what I am suggesting. We are proposing to use a Brain-Machine Interface (BMI).

Recent research in neuroprosthetics has been making some good progress recently. This consists of having a means to connect from automation to the human brain, in a relatively direct manner, formally known as BMI.

I realize this seems far-fetched. This is like some kind of science fiction story. Well, others are thinking that we are going to be soon seeing some exponential growth in our ability to create connections to the human mind. BMI is expected to be a huge growth industry with incredible market potential. I wouldn't count out the possibility.

Sure, today, the BMI connections are very crude. They are limited to simple reading of brain waves or electromagnetic pulses emitted by the brain. We don't know yet what those readings and pulses really mean in terms of the higher order thinking going on in the brain. Efforts to use the brain and machine connections are currently limited to aspects such as trying to make your mind blank versus trying to fill your mind with thoughts, and the connected device trying to read your mind senses perhaps that you are in one of those two states. This is very primitive, but at least promising.

Can BMI today read your inner most thoughts? No. Will it ever? We don't know. There are ethical discussions about whether or not we should let science take us that far. Maybe we should not have devices that could read our true thoughts. Will we lose a sense of personal privacy that we have taken for granted since the beginning of mankind? Will we potentially lose our sense of autonomy and maybe become locked into being connected with a device or automation.

Some are calling this BMI connection "brainjacking" and it is gradually emerging as a handy way to think about this topic. I suppose it is partially a misnomer in that we think of jacking something as a hijack of it. Humans might want to use these BMI devices, voluntarily, and for their own desired purposes. It would not then be a hijacking. It would be something that humans do because they wish to do so. Now, that being said, you might say that a variant would be circumstances whereby someone is being forced into allowing their brain to be hijacked by automation, in which case the term of brainjacking make be more sensible as a meaningful term.

How does this apply to self-driving cars?

I am glad you asked. We could potentially have a BMI device in a Level 4 self-driving car. Most of the time, the self-driving car and the AI are doing just fine. But, when the tough situations arise, namely the circumstances that we want to have a Level 5 self-driving car be able to do, in those instances, the Level 4 taps into the human mind to figure out how to properly handle the situation. We would potentially still consider the automation to be driving the car, since it is taking in the sensory data, it is analyzing it, it is relying commands to the controls of the car. The human that is connected mentally to the self-driving car is providing that last backstop, that final piece of the puzzle, being able to add cognitive power when needed.

You might wonder what is the difference between this aspect and simply having a human driver in the self-driving car that is ready to intervene. There are some differences.

First, the human driver that is ready to intervene is normally expected to be in the driver's seat and be ready to take the controls. Physically, they are positioned to take over the control of the vehicle. For the BMI connected human, they can be anywhere in the self-driving car and they are not physically accessing the controls of the car. They are purely added cognitive power for augmenting the AI. The AI has reached a juncture that it cannot "think its way out of" and needs to have the human to do so.

Second, the BMI connected driver could more readily be interacting with the AI of the self-driving car, in the sense that if the human in the vehicle wanted to alter the course of the car or change some other aspect, they could think it and convey as such to the AI. With the conventional approach of a human driver seated in the driver's seat, we are so far envisioning that they will be issuing verbal commands to the AI (see the chapter on in-car commands for self-driving cars). Verbal commands have their limitations due to the speed of being able to speak, the confusion over the use of words and what those words mean, etc.

Third, the human in the self-driving car does not necessarily need to have the physical aspects needed to drive the car, in the case of the BMI. This means that for example someone disabled that otherwise cannot drive a conventional car, could become a co-driver with the AI of the self-driving car. Or, perhaps someone that is elderly and has slowed reaction times and therefore is an unsafe driver if at the wheel. With the BMI approach, the physical aspects of the human don't particularly matter, since the AI and self-driving car will be doing all the physical aspects of driving.

The aforementioned approach does have its own downsides.

Suppose the BMI human that is connected to the self-driving car has an epileptic seizure. What does the AI do with this? Is the human trying to convey something to the AI about the car, or is it completely unrelated?

Similarly, how can the AI differentiate the thoughts in the head of the human? If I am a human in a self-driving car and have some kind of BMI connection, and I begin to daydream about race cars and going 120 miles per hour, suppose the AI of the self-driving car interprets this to suggest that I want the AI to push the car up to 120 mph and go car racing.

We'd have to have some perfected way of being able to mentally communicate to the AI of the self-driving car. Further, we'd need to have the AI be on its guard to not take commands that seem untoward. This is not just applicable to the BMI situation, but would be true for any circumstance wherein we are allowing a human occupant in the self-driving car to provide commands to the self-driving car. I've previously brought up that the human could be suicidal and use in-car verbal commands to tell the car to run over people. This is something we need to prevent, regardless if the commands are issued verbally or by some kind mental reading devices.

Another question arises about whom in the self-driving car can be BMI connected to the AI. So far, for levels 1 through 4 of a self-driving car, the human has to be someone that is able to drive a car. They need to be a licensed driver and qualified and valid to be able to drive a car. Would the BMI connected human need to also fit this definition? Some would say, yes, of course they need to be properly licensed as a driver since they are in a sense co-driving the vehicle. Others would say that no, they don't need to be licensed per se. If an elderly person that could not get their driver's license because of physical limitations and yet still has the mental capacity to reason and mentally drive a car, would they not be considered Okay as the co-driver?

The whole topic is raft with questions that involve societal issues. If the self-driving car crashes, who would be liable, the co-driving human or the AI? Would we even be able to discern which one was making the decisions about the driving of the car? Should the self-driving car maker be the one held responsible, since they provided the BMI capability to begin with? Will there be some enterprising entrepreneurs that opt to make a BMI device for co-driving of a self-driving car, and without permission from the maker of the self-driving car provide an add-on device that would allow the human BMI connection for co-driving?

Nobody yet knows any of this. We are very early on. But, there is a realistic possibility that we could have BMI connected devices, and we could use them in self-driving cars. For that aspect, I urge you to consider ways in which this can be done. In our lab, we've been toying with various crude mechanisms, and are eager to see how BMI evolves and then take this further along for self-driving cars. I suppose you could say that when it comes to driving a car, maybe two heads are better than one.

APPENDIX

APPENDIX A
TEACHING WITH THIS MATERIAL

The material in this book can be readily used either as a supplemental to other content for a class, or it can also be used as a core set of textbook material for a specialized class. Classes where this material is most likely used include any classes at the college or university level that want to augment the class by offering thought provoking and educational essays about AI and self-driving cars.

In particular, here are some aspects for class use:

o   <u>Computer Science</u>. Studying AI, autonomous vehicles, etc.

o   <u>Business</u>. Exploring technology and it adoption for business.

o   <u>Sociology</u>. Sociological views on the adoption and advancement of technology.

Specialized classes at the undergraduate and graduate level can also make use of this material.

For each chapter, consider whether you think the chapter provides material relevant to your course topic. There is plenty of opportunity to get the students thinking about the topic and force them to decide whether they agree or disagree with the points offered and positions taken. I would also encourage you to have the students do additional research beyond the chapter material presented (I provide next some suggested assignments they can do).

RESEARCH ASSIGNMENTS ON THESE TOPICS

Your students can find background material on these topics, doing so in various business and technical publications. I list below the top ranked AI related journals. For business publications, I would suggest the usual culprits such as the Harvard Business Review, Forbes, Fortune, WSJ, and the like.

Here are some suggestions of homework or projects that you could assign to students:

a) <u>Assignment for foundational AI research topic</u>: Research and prepare a paper and a presentation on a specific aspect of Deep AI, Machine Learning, ANN, etc. The paper should cite at least 3 reputable sources. Compare and contrast to what has been stated in this book.

b) <u>Assignment for the Self-Driving Car topic</u>: Research and prepare a paper and Self-Driving Cars. Cite at least 3 reputable sources and analyze the characterizations. Compare and contrast to what has been stated in this book.

c) <u>Assignment for a Business topic</u>: Research and prepare a paper and a presentation on businesses and advanced technology. What is hot, and what is not? Cite at least 3 reputable sources. Compare and contrast to the depictions in this book.

d) <u>Assignment to do a Startup:</u> Have the students prepare a paper about how they might startup a business in this realm. They must submit a sound Business Plan for the startup. They could also be asked to present their Business Plan and so should also have a presentation deck to coincide with it.

You can certainly adjust the aforementioned assignments to fit to your particular needs and the class structure. You'll notice that I ask for 3 reputable cited sources for the paper writing based assignments. I usually steer students toward "reputable" publications, since otherwise they will cite some oddball source that has no credentials other than that they happened to write something and post it onto the Internet. You can define "reputable" in whatever way you prefer, for example some faculty think Wikipedia is not reputable while others believe it is reputable and allow students to cite it.

The reason that I usually ask for at least 3 citations is that if the student only does one or two citations they usually settle on whatever they happened to find the fastest. By requiring three citations, it usually seems to force them to look around, explore, and end-up probably finding five or more, and then whittling it down to 3 that they will actually use.

I have not specified the length of their papers, and leave that to you to tell the students what you prefer. For each of those assignments, you could end-up with a short one to two pager, or you could do a dissertation length paper. Base the length on whatever best fits for your class, and the credit amount of the assignment within the context of the other grading metrics you'll be using for the class.

I mention in the assignments that they are to do a paper and prepare a presentation. I usually try to get students to present their work. This is a good practice for what they will do in the business world. Most of the time, they will be required to prepare an analysis and present it. If you don't have the class time or inclination to have the students present, then you can of course cut out the aspect of them putting together a presentation.

If you want to point students toward highly ranked journals in AI, here's a list of the top journals as reported by *various citation counts sources* (this list changes year to year):

o   Communications of the ACM

o   Artificial Intelligence

o   Cognitive Science

o   IEEE Transactions on Pattern Analysis and Machine Intelligence

o   Foundations and Trends in Machine Learning

o   Journal of Memory and Language

o   Cognitive Psychology

o   Neural Networks

o   IEEE Transactions on Neural Networks and Learning Systems

o   IEEE Intelligent Systems

o   Knowledge-based Systems

GUIDE TO USING THE CHAPTERS

For each of the chapters, I provide next some various ways to use the chapter material. You can assign the tasks as individual homework assignments, or the tasks can be used with team projects for the class. You can easily layout a series of assignments, such as indicating that the students are to do item "a" below for say Chapter 1, then "b" for the next chapter of the book, and so on.

a) What is the main point of the chapter and describe in your own words the significance of the topic,

b) Identify at least two aspects in the chapter that you agree with, and support your concurrence by providing at least one other outside researched item as support; make sure to explain your basis for disagreeing with the aspects,

c) Identify at least two aspects in the chapter that you disagree with, and support your disagreement by providing at least one other outside researched item as support; make sure to explain your basis for disagreeing with the aspects,

d) Find an aspect that was not covered in the chapter, doing so by conducting outside research, and then explain how that aspect ties into the chapter and what significance it brings to the topic,

e) Interview a specialist in industry about the topic of the chapter, collect from them their thoughts and opinions, and readdress the chapter by citing your source and how they compared and contrasted to the material,

f) Interview a relevant academic professor or researcher in a college or university about the topic of the chapter, collect from them their thoughts and opinions, and readdress the chapter by citing your source and how they compared and contrasted to the material,

g) Try to update a chapter by finding out the latest on the topic, and ascertain whether the issue or topic has now been solved or whether it is still being addressed, explain what you come up with.

The above are all ways in which you can get the students of your class involved in considering the material of a given chapter. You could mix things up by having one of those above assignments per each week, covering the chapters over the course of the semester or quarter.

As a reminder, here are the chapters of the book and you can select whichever chapters you find most valued for your particular class:

Companion Book By This Author

Advances in AI and Autonomous Vehicles: Cybernetic Self-Driving Cars

Practical Advances in Artificial Intelligence (AI) and Machine Learning
by
Dr. Lance B. Eliot, MBA, PhD

This title is available via Amazon and other book sellers

Companion Book By This Author

Self-Driving Cars:
"The Mother of All AI Projects"

by Dr. Lance B. Eliot, MBA, PhD

This title is available via Amazon and other book sellers

ABOUT THE AUTHOR

Dr. Lance B. Eliot, MBA, PhD is the CEO of Techbruim, Inc. and Executive Director of the Cybernetic Self-Driving Car Institute, and has over twenty years of industry experience including serving as a corporate officer in a billion dollar firm and was a Partner in a major executive services firm. He is also a serial entrepreneur having founded, ran, and sold several high-tech related businesses. He previously hosted the popular radio show *Technotrends* that was also available on American Airlines flights via their in-flight audio program. Author or co-author of ten books and over 300 articles, he has made appearances on CNN, and has been a frequent speaker at industry conferences.

A former professor at the University of Southern California (USC), he founded and led an innovative research lab on Artificial Intelligence in Business. Known as the "AI Insider" his writings on AI advances and trends has been widely read and cited. He also previously served on the faculty of the University of California Los Angeles (UCLA), and was a visiting professor at other major universities. He was elected to the International Board of the Society for Information Management (SIM), a prestigious association of over 3,000 high-tech executives worldwide.

He has performed extensive community service, including serving as Senior Science Adviser to the Vice Chair of the Congressional Committee on Science & Technology. He has served on the Board of the OC Science & Engineering Fair (OCSEF), where he is also has been a Grand Sweepstakes judge, and likewise served as a judge for the Intel International SEF (ISEF). He served as the Vice Chair of the Association for Computing Machinery (ACM) Chapter, a prestigious association of computer scientists. Dr. Eliot has been a shark tank judge for the USC Mark Stevens Center for Innovation on start-up pitch competitions, and served as a mentor for several incubators and accelerators in Silicon Valley and Silicon Beach. He serves on several Boards and Committees at USC, including having served on the Marshall Alumni Association (MAA) Board in Southern California.

Dr. Eliot holds a PhD from USC, MBA, and Bachelor's in Computer Science, and earned the CDP, CCP, CSP, CDE, and CISA certifications. Born and raised in Southern California, and having traveled and lived internationally, he enjoys scuba diving, surfing, and sailing.

ADDENDUM

Innovation and Thought Leadership in Self-Driving Driverless Cars

Practical Advances in Artificial Intelligence (AI) and Machine Learning

By

Dr. Lance B. Eliot, MBA, PhD

———

For supplemental materials of this book, visit:

www.lance-blog.com

For special orders of this book, contact:

LBE Press Publishing

Email: LBE.Press.Publishing@gmail.com